Thirsk

ffe

Husthwaite

or

dborough

ghbridge

River Ure

Great Ouseburn

Little Ouseburn

Nun Monkton

York

River Ouse

Wetherby

Leeds

NEW PASTURES
for a
YORKSHIRE
VET

To Lorraine,

Best wishes Julian Nort

JULIAN NORTON

GREAT N ORTHERN

Great Northern Books Limited
PO Box 1380, Bradford, BD5 5FB
www.greatnorthernbooks.co.uk

Every effort has been made to acknowledge correctly and contact the copyright
holders of material in this book. Great Northern Books Limited apologises for
any unintentional errors or omissions, which should be notified to the publisher.

ISBN: 978-1-914227-71-4

Design and layout: David Burrill

CIP Data
A catalogue for this book is available from the British Library

Contents

Foreword

Once upon a time, my veterinary life was simple. I lived and worked in the wonderful and quaint market town of Thirsk and treated pretty much all of the nearby animals. I was not an expert in anything, but a reasonable generalist and much of the enjoyment I gained from my vocation was because every day was different. At least, different in so far as there might be a predominance of cows (if it was pregnancy testing time at the point of housing in the autumn) or a multitude of lambing ewes in spring. It was varied but predictable and I never expected I'd be working anywhere else or doing anything differently.

But life sends us curveballs and over the last ten years there have been changes a-plenty. My last book (*Ruminations of a Yorkshire Vet*) described my weekly stories and experiences during the last period of almost three years in the even quainter market town of Boroughbridge, where I worked hard as an assistant. I felt more "Herriot" than ever. But that was another portion of my career and another change was coming.

After a piece of serendipity, I discovered a veterinary practice in Wetherby had suddenly closed its doors. It had once been a thriving business, filling a niche of veterinary care to animals around lower Wharfedale, Leeds and beyond. Recently bought out by a large conglomerate, it was evidently struggling and the only option had been, apparently, to shut up shop. Two or three new clients registered at Boroughbridge – seeking a new point of care for their pets – and I decided to go and investigate. I pulled up into the deserted car park early one morning before work. Peering into the windows, it seemed the practice had been suddenly abandoned. A solitary note on the door apologised to all the loyal clients for the unexpected news.

It was a fairly small unit, but modern. There was an adequate car park and the unit ticked a lot of boxes for me. Not least, it was a few minutes off one of the country's major trunk routes, with easy access to all the local towns and cities. I was immediately excited and set about more investigation. Would it be feasible? My boss at the Boroughbridge practice was not interested in taking it on as a kind of branch surgery, but I was hooked by its potential. I discovered the owner of the unit and arranged a meeting. The process was pretty simple and a team had been assembled. We knew the ingredients required to make a veterinary practice work well. No layers of middle management; no venture capital-backed owners; decent, approachable vets who would listen to owners and construct a sensible plan for tests and treatment.

In November 2019, Sandbeck Veterinary Centre opened. It was a step into the unknown. Would it work out? Would clients come to this new, well-placed but tucked-away building? Only time would tell. On day one, everyone waited with bated breath for the telephone to ring. It did. Eventually.

Most of the tales in this book – again, all originally published in *The Yorkshire Post* – relate to this new and exciting adventure, with old friends and colleagues, in pastures new.

Morning Caesar, Evening Caesar

I know I always seem to start this column with "it's been another busy week", or "my night on call was hectic", but Friday was busier and more hectic than usual and I make no excuses for being repetitive.

It all started first thing in the morning, with a whelping. The message that appeared on my phone before breakfast signified an early start – a basset hound was struggling to give birth and required a caesarean section. They were travelling from some distance away, so both I and the second-on-call vet had time for coffee and breakfast before we met at the practice to help bring new life into the world.

The op went incredibly well and, within the hour, there was a basketful of new pups. An early, but excellent, start to the day.

The rest of the day continued apace. It was my night on duty again and as evening surgery started, I was called to see a tup, who was having difficulty breathing. This special ram had been examined and treated the previous day, but the phone call told of an anxious farmer:

"I'm worried. He's a bit better but not much and he cost me a fortune! He's a belter of a tup and I just think he needs something else. Something a bit stronger."

I set off as the sun was heading towards the horizon, armed with bottles and syringes and hope. If the sheep had not improved much after the first round of treatment, the prognosis could be grave. Sheep, seemingly more than other animals, have a tendency either to live or die with not much in between.

But, when I arrived at the farm, the tup didn't seem too bad. He was standing up, but was puffing and blowing like a January-gym recruit who has recently been introduced to the treadmill. I hoped I could make him better. If not, the bright start to my day would be cancelled out. But the day wasn't over yet – my pocket was vibrating with another call!

"Can you go to see Tom – he has a cow to calve?" read the message on my phone. I knew exactly where to go and exactly which Tom it was. I was faced with a drive from Easingwold to just outside Harrogate, where the stricken cow and farmer were. I set off in a rush.

By now, the farm was even darker than the last and the patient was ten times as big, so I knew I was in for a long evening. I quickly realised she needed a caesarean and Tom was worried, both for his cow and for the state of his relationship.

"I'm supposed to be going out tonight with my girlfriend. It's her birthday and I promised. I'm already late. We should have set off an hour ago. She'll kill me!"

All I could do was apologise and crack on as quickly as I could. Under ideal circumstances (and I mean *ideal*), a cow caesarean can be completed by an experienced cattle vet in under an hour. Tonight, more than most, I needed to be quick and efficient, not just to save the calf and the mother but to rescue Tom's evening.

Luckily, the operation went like clockwork. The mother-to-be stood calmly and patiently whilst I made my incisions into her left flank. Fortune favoured us all as the calf was sitting easily in the left horn of the uterus, right under my incision. It landed, spluttering and slimy, in the darkness of the collecting yard. It had gone to plan and new life abounded – it had been a good day. A very good day. And, yes, the young couple did make it to the restaurant in time!

Weird Things this Week

Some odd things have happened this week.

"Julian. I have a hen to see this morning," explained my colleague, with a confused look on her face. "I've looked on the clinical notes. You saw it last time and you have written *it walks like John Cleese*."

She went on, "I wondered whether it was like this," and my colleague demonstrated one of the famous manoeuvres from the Ministry of Silly Walks, "or like this…" and she demonstrated another. It was the second walk that I'd had in mind in my notes. It wasn't even late enough in the day to be delirious through hypoglycaemia or exhaustion, yet we found ourselves laughing helplessly. A combination of general mickey-taking of my clinical notes, recollection of Monty Python jokes and the funny walks was just too much. I could – and should – compile a whole essay on amusing clinical notes one day.

The next odd thing was a dog. Its owner was extremely worried. Her beloved canine companion was in pain and had been for two days. Even worse, he had passed faeces in an unusual place. "He never usually goes there," she explained. I was less worried than the anxious owner, because I felt sure I would be able to ascertain the true cause. Going to the toilet in the wrong place might be odd, but there's usually a reason, so I set about my questions and examination. There was a very obvious point of pain halfway down the back, confirmed by shrieks and yelps.

"Has there been any accident that might have triggered this?" I asked.

"Well, yes," confirmed the anxious owner. "He was run into by a giant schnauzer whilst he was having a poo at the weekend. It was a hell-of-a-collision and my husband got covered in flying poo. It was terrible."

This was the crucial piece of information to slot into my diagnostic jigsaw, but possibly slightly more information than I really needed to know. At least it would remove the requirement for an X-ray investigation.

A peculiar cat appeared later the same day, with a condition called anisocoria. This is the word to describe the appearance of the pupils if they are disparate sizes. It has several causes, some serious. George, the elderly cat, seemed non-the-worse for his asymmetric pupils, but I called in our budding vet student (he had recently run the gauntlet of the hit-and-miss A-level assessment and been offered a place at vet school). Photos were taken and mental notes made of another unusual condition.

As the day drew to a close I thought it must be the end of the obscure and unusual, but as Fiona, our dynamic RVN, took a phone call, I could see her scribbling notes on a pad, with a concerned expression on her face. She had something else to add to this strange day, although not necessarily a veterinary task. I had just grabbed my gilet and headed for the door, hoping to get home in time for a quick bike ride before dark.

"Before you go, Julian, there's another message. It sounds quite serious. A farmer has just called. She's *lost* five cows. Three have been found in a field in Burton Leonard – they'd been walking down the road at one point, one has been found in a field of oil-seed rape and the other one has disappeared completely. What should I do?"

"Cows usually find a safe place," I replied. It wasn't really a veterinary issue. "They have a great self-preservation instinct. They'll find a neighbouring farm with cows, even if it involves jumping a fence. Anyway, I'm not on call and today has been too weird, so I'm going home."

D.A.

My afternoon plans had been changed abruptly so that I could operate on a cow. The first-time calver had not been right since she had delivered her calf and a colleague had been to examine her. The tell-tale pinging, just like a small stone being thrown at a metal bucket, heard down the stethoscope when the upper left side of the abdomen was flicked confirmed the diagnosis of a left displaced abomasum. This is a fairly common problem in cows soon after calving. When the large uterus, until recently full of calf, placenta and fluid, is suddenly empty there is a lot of spare space in the abdominal cavity. If the cow doesn't start eating immediately, the fourth stomach – the abomasum, which normally resides on the lower right part of the abdomen – can move and become trapped between the body wall and the huge rumen on the left. Further periods of poor appetite render it gassy, so it floats higher, making it even more trapped.

Luckily, an observant farmer spots the problem, suspects the diagnosis and calls the vet. An eagle-eared vet hears the ping and swaps stethoscope for scalpel. Or sends for a colleague to come with his scalpel, which is what happened this time – I was summoned to do the good bit. The surgery is very satisfying, often with instant results. The aim is to manipulate the abnormal abomasum back to its correct position and suture it in place so it doesn't float away again, like tethering a boat. There are a multitude of surgical options, but one of my favourites is to have two vets, one on each side of the patient, who stands patiently while first one vet, then the other feeds an arm inside the cow, passing the abomasum across the abdomen via a suture in its muscular wall. This is pushed into the waiting fingers of the second vet after a brief, abdominal handshake. It's simple and effective, but has the downside of needing two incisions and also two vets in the same place at the same time, which is often a challenge.

Another method involves just one vet. The cow is rolled onto her back, so the gas-filled abomasum floats back to approximately the correct position, whereupon it is fixed in place. It has the advantage of simplicity, but cows do not usually like lying upside down, so there is a concomitant struggle, with stray bovine feet flying in unpredictable directions, a great risk to vets and helpers.

A third technique, that is currently in favour, is the one I employed on this afternoon's cow. It has the advantage of needing only one vet and one incision. I made that incision on the right side of the abdomen, then reached in and across, past the rumen to find the gas-filled abomasum hiding behind it. With some difficulty, I squeezed the gas out so that I could pull the abomasum back to its correct place. There is a piece of fat attached to it that acts as a very useful landmark and a handy tab to grab and suture. It's called the lesser omentum, or more affectionately the "sow's ear", because that is what it looks like. When this appears at the incision, I know I've got the right bit. I swiftly attached the sow's ear to the inside of the cow and, forty minutes after I'd started, I was the washing blood from my arm and the cow was walking back to the field. I hung around for a few more minutes to watch her progress.

"I know what you're waiting for," said the farmer, impressed in an understated way at the simplicity of the technique. "It'll make your day if she puts her head down and takes a mouthful of grass."

Testing, Testing 1,2,3

Unlike Mr Hancock, I've been doing a lot of testing this week. Some tests have been diagnostic – a biochemistry profile for a dog with no appetite and a Cushing's disease test for a schnauzer with an excessive thirst. Others have been screening tests, where a large population of healthy, asymptomatic animals are sampled to check for the occult presence of disease within that population. This week's case was a flock of extremely beautiful, pedigree sheep. The test was useful for the sheep but, arguably, not the best use of a pathology lab's time and skills, given the current, more pressing, circumstances.

I arrived on the farm in good time. There were just over a hundred sheep to sample, which I expected would be a morning's work, although I've learnt from experience that, even for an expert sampler, things can go horribly wrong. There is a knack to blood-sampling sheep, because they are covered in thick wool and resistant to standing still and the task can send an inexperienced vet into panic. I once went to rescue a tearful junior colleague who, after four hours and with a growing pile of spoiled tubes and bent needles, had managed to test only a handful of ewes. But I learnt the skill in my first job in the north of Scotland, where we'd test hundreds and hundreds of sheep to ensure they were free of a disease called Enzootic Abortion, so I got quite good. It's a pleasant job, even though the thighs burn after a few hours of the repetitive squats required to sample every animal.

The Suffolks were behaving impeccably and everything was progressing smoothly, until one boisterous shearling took off vertically, clearing the gate and landing on the table where my equipment was arranged, scattering tubes and paperwork everywhere. The farmer's mobile phone, which was also on the table, landed in a bucket of water with a plop. Luckily, since blood tubes are now plastic rather than glass, and since the phone was in an excellent waterproof case, the accident was not as catastrophic as it might have been.

As we got towards the last few in the group, the farmer announced, "Right, there's some more ewes at the other farm." These were not the words I wanted to hear just before lunch, when I thought I'd finished. On the other farm, the sheep were still grazing happily in the field. I watched as the farmer summoned two hapless looking collies to help bring them in.

Shouts of "come by," were quickly followed by "come back," as the two dogs charged around the field, but eventually the sheep were in one place and the final blood samples were collected. On the way home, listening to the radio reports about the woeful statistics and false hope of COVID testing in the UK, I pondered the expected results for the sheep (and the limitations of screening tests in general). Mass testing should reveal the population of healthy sheep to be clear. But not all tests are 100% accurate, with potential for false positives and false negatives, which is a big problem for large-scale population screening. A good screening test should pick up *all* possible cases, including those that are pre-clinical or asymptomatic, but runs the very real risk of giving false positive results. Even with a sensitivity of 99%, out of 10 million "moon shot" COVID tests, for example, there could be 100,000 false positive results, with goodness knows what lockdown or isolation consequences. Almost as bad are the false negatives, where a false sense of security is given to a carrier or shedder. I parcelled up my own blood tubes securely in polystyrene boxes and labelled them clearly as "biological samples", hoping for everyone's sake there would be no positive results, true or false.

Last Weekend on Call

For the last twenty-five years, planning a weekend away has necessitated an in-depth scrutiny of the rota, in an attempt to predict how the weekend duties will pan out. There are always two questions; am I on duty and, if I am, is there anyone with whom I could arrange a simple swap? This brings the issue of whether anyone else needs to be off that weekend, or if a colleague is away on holiday. In a smallish veterinary practice, there is never any guarantee of being able to make a social occasion, attend an important family event or significant engagement. A compromised life away from work is something to which most veterinary surgeons become accustomed. I'm not sure if the disappointed family ever completely reconciles the conflicting pulls of normal life and ongoing on-call commitments.

However, I can now say with certainty that there will be definitely *no* clash with a busy weekend rota and the important upcoming event, involving all members of my close family. Because I have just completed my final weekend on call, at least for the foreseeable future. Once, this would have invoked feelings of being a skiver, shirking my share of the work and not pulling my weight within the practice team, but a quick calculation revealed that this was approximately the six hundredth weekend of my career, on call, with a beeper in my pocket, at the mercy of emergencies, which I reckon is more than sufficient. I can't wait for the shift to my shifts.

The weekend in question was anticlimactic. Saturday was a quiet day, the highlight of which was two successive – but unrelated – clients who had the same surname. One had a rabbit that had stopped eating and the other a cat with an abscess on its head. Sunday was more eventful and saw me performing a post-mortem on a recently deceased tup, treating a horse with choke and visiting a pony, at 10.30 at night which, a bit like me, had only eaten half of its tea.

But I've had some shockers over the years, full of attrition as well as adrenalin-fuelled dramas. It's not the working of a weekend *per se* that's hard. Work is work, whatever the day of the week. It's the fact that a normal week precedes the seventy-two-hour stint and an equally full week follows. There's sometimes a half-day off the following Monday, if you're lucky, but not if you're not – I've just finished a run of twenty-six days of working without a day off, due to various swaps and rearrangements. By the end of a run like that, instead of using any free time to go on a long bike ride, see your family or pursue your hobbies, you end up asleep on the sofa.

One ridiculous, super-Saturday some years ago, I performed three bitch caesarean sections, completing the final one in a state of semi-consciousness at midnight. At the start of my career, when farm calls were much more frequent, I had thirteen calls in one Sunday, four of which were to treat the same cow. But it is being repeatedly woken up that wears you down the most. A terrible Sunday night in March had me replacing the uterus in three cows, on three different farms at exactly two-hour intervals. I was not in a good state to start another busy week on Monday morning.

The end of my weekends on call might mark the end of an era. I prefer to see it as the start of a new one, a little further down the A1 to the banks of another marvellous Yorkshire river, where many more, exciting veterinary challenges lie ahead.

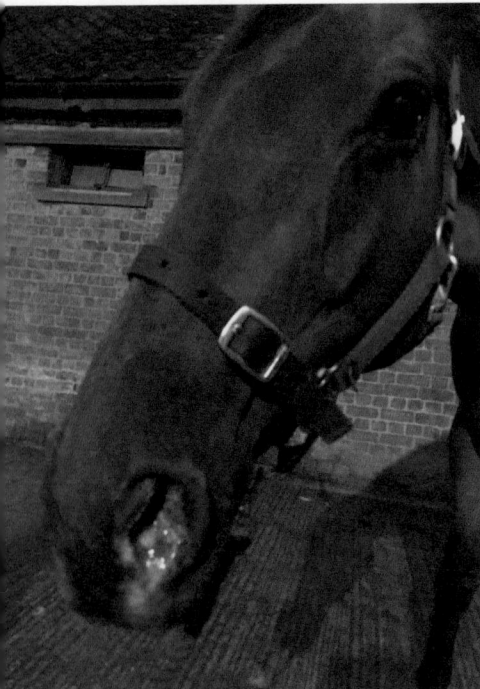

Horse with the ugly nasal discharge connected with choke.

Wrapping Cats and All Creatures

In many ways, veterinary practice has not changed much over the decades. Watching the current Channel 5 remake of *All Creatures Great and Small*, it is abundantly evident that some things are exactly the same: cows needed to be calved back then in exactly the same way as they do now. The same bugs caused mastitis in Herriot's day as today, although admittedly there are now powerful and effective antimicrobials available to quell the infection, as long as the dairy company allows it. We've advanced in some areas, but I'm certain there are still bottles of potions and ointments on the shelves of many large animal practices across the country reminding vets of days gone by. Personally, I've mostly refrained from exploring these ancient remedies but have been tempted, on occasions, by Friars Balsam. Huge buckets of Udder Salve can also look tempting to smear on an inflamed udder, but the brown bottle I found containing small and ominously blue oblong tablets remained very much off limits. On its label, the scrawled words *For Stupefying Pigeons*, without any reference to the drug, its concentration or its contraindications did nothing to fill a modern practitioner with confidence about the provenance of the tablets.

Some years ago, when various antediluvian veterinary relics started to arrive at the practice where I worked, en route to a local museum, the senior partner could be found sifting through the rusty antiques, muttering to himself, "That's a good 'un. We'll keep that." It was a measure of how little some aspects of the profession had advanced.

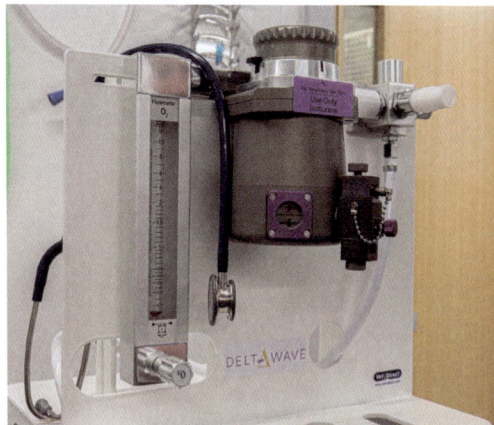

But in other ways, things are very different nowadays.

In many ways, veterinary practice has advanced on a par with human medicine.

Modern advances, many enthusiastically borrowed from our medical cousins, have swamped the profession. MRI machines, for example, once regarded with suspicion (mostly because no one knew how to interpret the images) can now be found within half an hour's travel of most first opinion practices and are available, at a price, to aid (or confuse) the diagnosis of any condition.

Veterinary anaesthesia, and the monitoring thereof, has developed to be on a par with human anaesthesia, which is a very good thing. Vets can now happily tackle a "general" with confidence rather than anxiety, even in an elderly cat. When I first started my career, it was not uncommon for some vets to take a different approach altogether. Occasionally, when a geriatric cat was in need of some dental work, the procedure on the ops list said *cat dental- wrap cat*. At first, I could not understand what this meant. Wrapping a cat? Did that mean sternly reprimanding it, maybe by a smack on the knuckles? Making it into a present? Or maybe singing a wordy song? Closer questioning revealed it to be the old-fashioned and, quite frankly, cruel practice of enveloping the poor cat in a towel so it couldn't struggle, while any loose teeth were swiftly extracted. The theory was that the job was quick and simple and, if the cat was held still, could be completed without the need for (in those days potentially quite dangerous) general anaesthesia. It might have been an accepted procedure in Herriot's day, when a cat was regarded as nothing more than a catcher of vermin, and when anaesthetics were not so safe but, even twenty-five years ago, there was no place for such a practice. And all vets, at some point in their career, have been persuaded by an anxious owner to "remove a lump under local", to avoid a possibly dangerous GA. It usually doesn't go smoothly.

So, yes, we can love to love the old stories and reflect with a warm glow about those halcyon, brown-coated veterinary days, but give me modern practice, precise X-rays, defined diagnoses, quality analgesics and accurate monitoring of my patients any day.

Fell Gather

"Would you be free next week to come and help round up some sheep on a big hill in the Lake District?"

It was hard to know how to answer that question. I knew it would be for the popular new Channel 5 series *Friday on the Farm* and I knew it could be an ephemeral offer, with potential to be changed or cancelled within a day or so, subject to the vagaries of normal life, farmers' commitments and the whims of the TV world. I also knew that if I could swap a duty and get there on time, and if the weather was right, it would be something that could be a lot of fun.

So, of course, without hesitation, I agreed.

The trip up to Buttermere was a familiar one. As a young assistant, working in Thirsk, I would make the journey on a free weekend or even when a sunny day coincided with an afternoon off. With my mountain bike packed in the back seat, I could drive across the A66, reassemble the bike, cycle up and down Helvellyn, and drive home. I could be back just in time for last orders at the Blacksmith's Arms. But this time, twenty years later, I'd be staying overnight in the Lakes, rather than rushing home.

I met up with Eddie, the young shepherd, and his mates, each of whom was replete with a bunch of two or three rough-looking (but very fit) dogs, who would be helping gather the sheep from the fell.

I had helped collect sheep like this once before, when I was a vet student learning the ropes of animal husbandry at a fantastic family farm in Threshfield. The gimmer lambs were separated from the rest of the flock, dipped and then sent to the sales to provide the robust basis of lowland flocks. The ewes were sorted, to check their fitness to survive another year on the fell, nurturing a pair of lambs in all weathers. I loved it, not only from the farming perspective but because it made me feel as if I was part of the fabric and tradition of the hills.

So, setting off with Eddie and his hefted mates rekindled some halcyon memories. It was no understatement to say that Eddie and his Lakeland farming friends were as hefted as the Herdwick sheep, whose DNA was so intrinsically entwined with every contour, gill and crag of the fells where they lived. Born and brought up on those fells, the farmers knew the landscape as well as the sheep, who had no need for stonewalls to keep them contained.

As we climbed higher, Eddie explained the plan: one by one his helpers would peel off with their dogs to head off the sheep before the pass. Eddie and I, with his lean pack of faithful dogs, climbed and climbed, almost to the top of the crags that marked the extent of the grazing area. Views of Crummock Water opened up, with giants like Red Pike behind and the Irish Sea and Dumfries even further away. They took my breath away. We paused periodically, not so much to regain our breath or to admire the view, but to look for sheep dotted, as they were, all over the fell and to ensure the dogs didn't miss any. Eventually, as the dog teams came together, all the sheep on the hill were funnelled down to the bottom of the steep-sloping hillside, towards the farm below.

It had been a great day and a privilege to help Eddie gather his sheep. I resolved not to leave it so long before I returned to the Lakes.

Return to the Lakes

My trip to help Eddie, the young farmer with a passion for the fells and his flock of Herdwicks, made me resolve not to leave it too long before I returned to the Lake District. I'd forgotten how beautiful it was with its huge, bulky peaks, waterfalls and endless variety of textures as rocky crags and brown, bracken-covered upper slopes give way to a deeper green where the grass grows. A perennial presence, oblivious to coronavirus restrictions, sunshine or torrential rain, are the Herdwick sheep, which are, literally, everywhere. They are very different to the familiar lowland breeds, which bulk up to provide tasty chops and Sunday dinners. Herdwicks have strong, sturdy legs. Their faces are fuzzy, like a bearded mountain man and the blackness of their lamb fleece turns grey after just a few years. The harshness of life on the mountains must accentuate the aging process. When gathered together, a flock of Herdwicks with their lambs take on a thousand different shades.

So, I was keen to get back to explore. The combination of a new life with not so many weekend work commitments and the COVID-19 related abolition of the normally rammed sporting calendar for my kids, gave Jack (my eldest son) and me the perfect opportunity. The forecast was for dry but windy weather and we hatched a plan to embark upon an excellent adventure. The campervan was quickly packed, with bikes loaded on the back and energy-rich foods shoved inside. Jack and I were heading to Langdale to attempt the iconic cycling route called the "Fred Whitton".

This is a classic and very hard cycling loop, covering 180 kilometres and climbing around 3,500 metres, including the steepest and hardest mountain pass in the UK – Hardknott Pass. It was a spur-of-the-moment decision, which are usually the best. But it meant that we hadn't had the chance to prepare properly, either mentally or physically. But we were fit, ambitious and full of enthusiasm, which I reckoned would be enough. What I lacked in youthful energy, I made up for with accumulated endurance, experience and energy-dense adipose tissue, all of which I've been working on for years.

The altitude map across the whole route looked similar to the COVID-19 graphs that adorn the news every five minutes, with terrible spikes and peaks rearing up vertically, promising wave after wave of maximum heart rate and eyes stinging with sweat. It started with Kirkstone Pass, steep and ongoing, but simple enough and we whizzed down happily, having ticked off the first of nineteen climbs. As we zipped through Glenridding, four Herdwick sheep stood at a bus stop. At least I thought so. Maybe I was already hypoglycaemic and hallucinating.

Honister Pass was the next biggie, before we zoomed down, right past Eddie's farm in Buttermere. Sadly, there was no time to call for a cup of tea, because Newlands Pass demanded our attention as it cut its way, at 25% (again), diagonally up the flank of Robinson Fell. From here, as long as my vision was not blurred by sweat, I could see exactly where I'd been to gather the sheep a few weeks earlier. They were back up on the fells now, in splendid isolation. Next was Whinlatter, gentle by comparison, before we turned south along the western edge of the Lakes. Sellafield nuclear reprocessing plant appeared in the distance, in the last throes of being decommissioned, with hundreds of offshore windmills whirring round beyond. It aptly summed up the UK's changing energy provision, but we didn't have time to discuss the evolution of power. We had our own power output to consider, because the menacing threats of Hardknott and Wrynose beckoned.

First Day: Smiley Happy People

It had been a good first day – action-packed, successful and rewarding. I sensed that this might be the start of something amazing and, beaming to myself, I sang loudly to the tunes from my car radio as I drove home. Our new clinic was smart, spotless and modern. Everything was exactly where it was supposed to be. The ultrasound scanner, with its state-of-the-art colour flow Doppler (to measure the blood flow through vessels and across valves) had its own room, so too the X-ray machine and digital processor. The dental suite even had its very own dental X-ray unit, because teeth need a specialised machine to take their pictures. Dogs and cats had separate kennel areas and we'd even planned a colour-coded bedding system – blue for dogs and pink for cats.

First thing in the morning, after rummaging through cupboards to find where everything lived, I drew up my pre-medication doses and pondered the ops list ahead of me. The list on the board looked like the surgery examination in my veterinary finals, comprising various long and complicated-sounding procedures. *Rostral hemi-mandibulectomy – remove acanthomatous ameloblastoma* was the longest and most serious sounding surgery, but *rhinoplasty/ soft palate resection to treat Brachiocephalic Obstructive Airway Syndrome* and *keratectomy to treat corneal dermoid* (second and third on the list, respectively) were almost as impressive. But as well as being full of wonderful words – and more importantly – my list was full of brilliant patients.

Lola, the French bulldog, snuffled in with enthusiasm, despite her narrow nostrils and elongated soft palate, both of which seriously compromised her ability to breathe freely. Later that day, she left with a much more suitable upper airway, her nostrils widened to let the fresh air flood in. The back of her throat was more normal too, without the excess tissue that had caused all the flapping, flopping and snoring. She should be ready to run a marathon soon, we joked as she boarded her ride home.

Cola the Shih Tzu puppy was next, with a similar-sounding name but a very different problem – an abnormal, hairy structure called a *dermoid* protruding from the surface of her left eyeball. It looked as out of place and ugly as it sounded. It would have been fairly ugly even if it was on her skin, but growing out of the middle of the cornea, the unusual structure was making the puppy's eye sore and watery as well as obscuring her vision.

Amy, the Labrador with the problematic jaw, did not stop wagging her tail from the moment she arrived at our new practice. I think she was impressed.

"Will you do a mandibular nerve block?" asked Mark, my colleague. Mark and I are old mates from school, when we spent many summer holidays together, exploring the mountains of northern Europe, camping by lakes and traversing icecaps. Now, thirty years on, we have joined forces again. Mark knows a lot about advanced dental procedures and showed me how to numb the main nerve that provides sensation to the lower jaw – the site of Amy's tumour. Until now, most of the nerve blocks I'd performed were to allow me to disbud a calf or dehorn a cow, so this was new to me.

"Instil a couple of mils just where the nerve emerges from the foramen, medial to the ventral mandibular ramus," he explained. With my mandibular nerve block on board, Amy came round from her anaesthetic pain and tumour-free, and immediately started to wag her tail again.

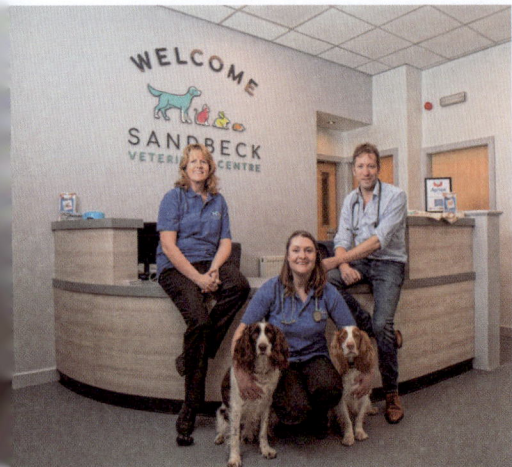

Three happy patients with relieved owners is usually enough to make for a rewarding day. But my first day was even better, because I'd learnt a new trick.

Photo Courtesy of Roth Read Photography.

Cowpox, PCR and Vaccines

Jessie the cat looked pretty awful and her owner was worried. She had a horribly infected foot and her previous vet had suggested the solution might be to amputate the leg. But Jessie's foot was only part of the problem because she also had scabby, sore and bleeding lesions all over her body, head and face. Biopsies were required and I took her to theatre immediately to take little samples of her skin. The lab could do their thing and use powerful microscopes and skill to make a definitive diagnosis. I had my suspicions about the cause of Jessie's lesions and we awaited the lab report with trepidation.

Usually, results come by email, but a couple of days later the pathologist left an urgent message on my phone wanting to talk about the results. He even gave his mobile number, so I knew the findings must be unusual. The last time I spoke by mobile phone with a pathologist about a complicated case was a few years ago, when I was treating a collie with a rare bone marrow condition. Emailed pictures from down the microscope whizzed across the Atlantic for an expert's opinion and I found myself talking to an American professor of clinical pathology. We were both away from our workplaces: my end of the in-depth cytological discussion was conducted by the frozen peas in Tesco. She was in Walmart in downtown Philadelphia.

In Jessie's case, my tentative diagnosis of pemphigus foliaceus, a rare condition in itself, turned out to be (in all probability) completely wrong. The pathologist explained the nature of the lesions – cutaneous necrosis, intense exudative and neutrophilic inflammation. He suspected a different diagnosis altogether: cowpox!

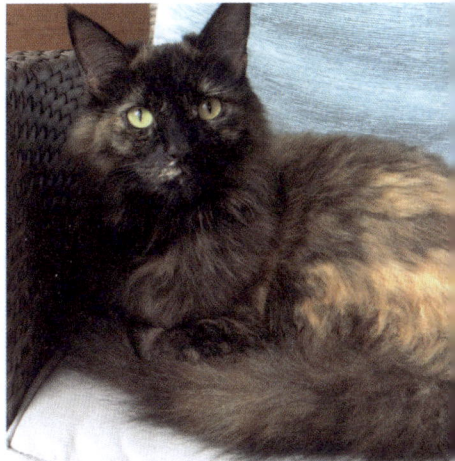

Jessie, in a pre-virus state of beautiful health.

This is also rare and he went on to explain that feline cowpox usually appeared as a single lesion, often on the foot, and then spread, after a ten-day period of incubation and viraemia, to cause lesions all over the cat's surface. "We need to do a PCR test to confirm, though," he added. It was a sentence with which everyone amidst COVID-19 has become very familiar.

Whilst unusual, the appearance of cowpox seemed apt. At a time when the world anxiously awaits the development of a novel vaccine for coronavirus, it was the cowpox virus that led Edward Jenner to discover the concept of vaccination. Way back in 1796, this pioneering scientist was decades ahead of his time. He discovered that milkmaids, who had been exposed to the relatively mild cowpox infection from milking affected cows, were immune to the genuinely deadly effects of the smallpox virus. Cowpox served as an effective natural vaccine until a modern vaccine was created in the nineteenth century. It was a huge success and, following a World Health Organization campaign in the sixties and seventies, smallpox achieved the status of being the only global human disease to be eradicated. This evidence – that clever science and a coordinated strategy can save the day – should buoy us all in these stricken times.

Smallpox is gone, but evidently cowpox persists and, although now uncommon in cows, voles and rodents can carry it around. It turned out that Jessie had caught a rat a few weeks before and we assumed this to be the source of infection. Whilst awaiting the PCR results, Jessie was following strict "self" isolation to avoid spreading her infection more widely. But there was another discussion to be had with Jessie's owner, following the revelation and pending PCR confirmation.

"And cowpox is contagious to people, so you'll need to exercise proper hygiene precautions," I explained. This bit was easy because nowadays we all know how to rid our skin of pesky virus particles: get the soap and start singing "Happy birthday."

Fox Poo and a Decomposing Porpoise

A fraught text message told the story of a domestic crisis last Saturday. Anne had been running in the woods with Emmy, our Jack Russell:

Can you get the baby bath from the garage and fill it with warm, soapy water. The dog's just found fox poo and she's covered.

The message wasn't in capitals, but it may as well have been. A text message, or worse an email, spelt out in capitals is always a bad thing – somehow it conveys the seriousness of a situation even more than shouting.

I readied the required equipment. The baby bath, which I found in the garage, had a crack in it but, nevertheless, I filled it to the brim with warm water that was VERY soapy (note the capitals). An anxious Anne and a smelly, but rather pleased with herself Emmy emerged from the car, both at high speed – Emmy rushing to greet me, proudly showing off her new aroma and her delightful new shade of greenish-brown, Anne sprinting to get hold of her before she jumped on me or burst into the kitchen, where her new perfume would be spread around the inside of the otherwise spotless and neutral-smelling house.

Why do dogs do this?

It must be something to do with territories – or maybe an attempt at a disguise.

Eventually, Emmy was Persil-white and bouffant after her garden bath and considerably less smelly, so it was not the end of the world that it might have been. It reminded me of a time, a couple of years ago on the long, straight beach of Sandsend, when a golden retriever performed a similar trick with the beached carcass of a decomposing porpoise. The scene was so disgusting that it should not be described in much detail, for fear of frightening readers and putting people off their breakfast. The dog's owners spotted the potential problem in advance and secured the retriever safely on his lead, much to his annoyance. But the dog had already sniffed the air and sensed the fun that could be had with a decomposing animal, its smell much worse than fox faeces. After having passed the porpoise and reached, what the owners perceived to be, a safe and sensible distance, they let the golden retriever off his lead again, only to watch in horror as he turned tail and charged back at breakneck speed to plunge himself into the rotting mess for his best ever roll. In unison, all the watching dog walkers on the beach reeled in repugnance (but also relief that it wasn't their dog).

There is a corollary to dead porpoises and fox poo stories – another odiferous danger, of which I've just become aware. This comes in the form of hedgehog faeces. We've had a family of hedgehogs living in our garden, munching on slugs and worms. We have enjoyed watching them stomp round the garden on their evening rounds. It turns out, however, that hedgehog poo is just as appealing as fox poo to a dog who is intent on disguising herself. Emmy can find the poo in all corners of the garden – under bushes and leaves. She assumes a pose very similar to the "downward dog" that yoga enthusiasts adopt and places the top of her head firmly on top of the slimline poo. It happens to be exactly the part of her

head that you'd pat. Next, she rubs vigorously, embedding the smell into the skin as well as her hair. Then, she trots into the kitchen!

Normally, Emmy's behaviour and endearing charm are beyond reproach, but her persistent and recent habit of poo-rolling is becoming rather annoying. Luckily, the hedgehogs are now hibernating!

Smelly Emmy.

Celebrity Bottom Drawer

After a series of emails a few weeks ago, my life has taken a turn for the even more strange. The first email came from the renowned percussionist Evelyn Glennie, with whom I had recently recorded a podcast, and she was inviting me to participate in a charity event.

Hi Julian, I hope you don't mind me bothering you, but I got this email request yesterday and thought you might be able to take part, she wrote.

The planned event was to consist of an online, COVID-safe auction in aid of the East Anglia Children's Hospices. The call had gone out to anyone who might have old or unwanted bric-a-brac that someone somewhere might like to buy. It was to be called *Celebrity Bottom Drawer*. The level of strangeness escalated when I noticed the organiser of the event was no other than Griff Rhys Jones, who needs no introduction. I emailed him and explained that I was a vet and, while I was on TV, I probably didn't qualify to take part since I was contrary to Evelyn's assertion – a celebrity. It wasn't long before a reply appeared in my inbox. Actual Griff Rhys Jones reassured me that eleven series of *The Yorkshire Vet* was more than enough to put me in the running and so I confirmed that I was happy to help. I had a selection of first-edition James Herriot books and I could sneak in a collection of my own first editions. By chance, a friend had recently given me a quirky wooden planter in the shape of a pig, complete with drawn-on eyes and mouth and cut-out-and-screwed-on ears, specifically for the purpose of donating to a raffle or similar fundraising occasion.

griffrhysjones

Filled with books, this seemed the perfect unusual lot for the auction.

Griff was delighted – he found the book–pig planter combo amusing and appealing. I could almost imagine the scene in *Not the Nine O'Clock News*, with Rowan Atkinson pulling funny faces and Mel Smith being exasperated as they unwrapped the parcel to reveal books inside a wooden pig.

Anyhow, I packaged it all up and sent it by special delivery last Friday. I confirmed to Griff that the pig had flown. However, as the days pass and posts from *@celebritybottomdrawer* appear on my Instagram feed, my feeling of embarrassment grows. Each day, another of the various and generous donors pops up with a handsome or beautiful smiling face. The procession of A-listers started with some big guns; David Walliams was followed by Dawn French (who had generously donated a Rolex watch). Next was Davina McCall (offering *that* dress), swiftly followed by Ant and Dec. I sweated uncomfortably, as I felt increasingly out of place. It wasn't helped when Nigella Lawson smiled seductively to show her support for the charity (I was delighted to see she, too, was offering a book – although only one).

The faces that followed were like a roll call from the red carpet. Ralph Fiennes, Matt Lucas (he was donating a potato), Lee Mack and Joanna Lumley. It was hard to know what they would do with me – surely there wouldn't be time or space for *every* donor to be put on display? As David Schwimmer followed Olivia Colman and Emma Thompson, it seemed as if they were saving the best until last, although an antediluvian tennis racket from Nigel Havers surely did not beat Sir Paul McCartney's offering.

We all wait, with bated breath and crossed fingers, to see how much can be raised for the brilliant charity. And if anyone fancies a wooden pig, filled with books about veterinary stories, past and present, you know where you can get one (please)!

Old Farmers, Old Stories

Several weeks ago, I had a very simple job: injecting a young heifer that had, twenty-eight days previously, accidentally encountered a bull. A pregnancy was neither wanted nor planned, so it was the bovine equivalent of the morning-after pill, although it wasn't a pill and it wasn't the morning after. On this sunny, late autumnal morning when both vet and farmer had finished almost all of their routine jobs, there was time to chat about the present, and the future and to reminisce about the past. I love looking forward, always with optimism and excitement (tomorrow will always be an improvement on today) but sharing past experiences and stories is almost as good. Especially when the stories come from a wise, old Yorkshire farmer.

We touched on the best (and worst) of the previous vets who had been on the farm over recent decades. Vic Bean featured top of the pile, which was only fitting because he was a magnificent vet and an amazing man.

"He came one day to see my sheep," recounted the farmer.

"They weren't looking so good, so I asked him to have a look at them. He filled his pipe and puffed away, just looking at the way they ate and moved. After a while, Vic said he suspected liver fluke and would like to do a post-mortem." The farmer recounted, still visibly in awe, all these years later.

"And within minutes, without taking the pipe out of his mouth, he'd opened up a ewe which had just died, sliced into its liver and found some. 'Look at the buggers, they are still moving', he said and I still remember that day. What a vet, what a man!"

I could only agree. I'd met Vic a few times. Once was outside the old veterinary investigation centre in Thirsk, at the start of my veterinary career. We were both dropping off samples and we chatted in the car park outside. He was a veterinary surgeon with many years of experience and I was a novice junior. Yet he addressed me as an equal; something I'll never forget.

More stories from the past quickly followed and the old farmer recounted the time when he was young, when he had helped a friend, Bill Merrin from Nether Silton, whose colt needed gelding. Alf White, another master vet, came to do the honours.

"We got the horse and he put this great big, clumsy canvas bag over his head. Then, he poured some liquid – I think it was chloroform – into the bottom and he left the horse to wander around until it fell over, asleep. Then he said, 'Right, you and Colin kneel on his neck, to stop him getting up'. And that's what we did."

I could picture the scene. Although I have never used chloroform to anaesthetise a horse, I have heard many similar stories. I've placed enough horses under GA to know exactly the concern and the sense of drama.

"'Are you nearly done up at that end, Vet'nary?' I shouted," continued the farmer as he recounted his story in detail.

"'Not quite, why – is everything OK?' Alf apparently replied.

'Not really,' I called from the head/neck end of the horse. 'Colin's fallen asleep!'"

Poor old Colin, attending to his task with fervour, must have got too close to the chloroform-filled mask and breathed too deeply, rendering him as stupefied as the colt. This old-fashioned drug was highly effective, in humans as well as horses.

I felt like I could (and should) have spent a few more hours chatting with this funny, old farmer and enjoying his stories. But time was ticking on again. My phone was ringing and I had another job to do…

Reflections on the Rivers

I've always been fascinated by the rivers of Yorkshire. It might be because I was born and brought up a stone's throw from the mighty Calder, the thoroughfare that was once the life force of West Yorkshire's industrial heritage. I've watched barges trundle past – even in my lifetime they were piled high with coal – and wondered at the mysterious oxbow lakes, past which I walked with our lurcher and my dad or grandfather.

I wonder if a river and its characteristics have a bearing on the mood and ambience of the towns and villages along its course? I'm sure the slow, laconic wandering of the Ure through Boroughbridge must have lent some of its serenity to the town. Once Boroughbridge was a major transport hub, offering rest, sustenance and accommodation to travellers and horses. Before that, the Ure was a significant link in the trade of wool from Fountains Abbey to the Humber and beyond to Italy and Belgium. Nowadays, everything in the town seems to progress at the same pace as the Ure. Yes, there are brief moments of excitement: the weir is so full of energy, and its nearby residents once so full of foresight, that electricity was generated by the Boroughbridge and District Electrical Company, decades before the National Grid was developed.

Further north, the half-hearted attempt to canalise Thirsk's little river – Cod Beck – to improve the town's connectivity to the Swale, which began in 1767 and was abandoned soon after when the railway arrived, reminds Thirsk and Sowerby dog walkers that chances must be seized at the opportune moment. Meanwhile, the beck, which starts above Osmotherley, steadily attempts to return to its original, willow-lined course. Slow and steady, a bit like the town, it might eventually get there.

The Swale, which takes its name from the Anglo-Saxon word *Sualuae*, which aptly means "rapid and prone to deluge", is more dramatic and its upper reaches are full of industrial history dating back much further than canals. The Romans mined lead from the hills overlooking its dale. After sudden and heavy deluges sediment containing lead ores are often deposited on the flooded fields further downstream. I've seen numerous cases of lead poisoning in cattle and sheep grazing on recently-flooded pastures as stock have inadvertently ingested the toxic-heavy metal. The Swale certainly leaves its mark!

Recently, following the opening of my new vet practice in Wetherby – a serendipitous opportunity involving an old friend and a former colleague – I've found myself becoming reacquainted with another old friend – the river Wharfe. As a teenager, I spent many weekends running along its banks, honing my cross-country endurance. By the time the Wharfe arrives at Wetherby, it has lots of tales to tell. The hectic turmoil of the Strid gives way to more gentle sections, flanked by pastures of grazing sheep. Optimistic fishermen stand knee-deep in an attempt to outwit trout. It has picked up a peaty tinge, probably more so than other Yorkshire rivers, so it looks like strong, milk-less tea. It has witnessed the history of a 12th-century Augustinian monastery, irrigated fish farms and tempted ambitious kids across stepping-stones. I swam in it once, racing in one of my early triathlons. Near the halfway point, when swimmers had to circumnavigate a buoy that indicated a change of direction, I was overtaken by a competitor. I swam, in my mind heroically, but in practice hectically. He was walking and he strode past me through the now shallow water at much greater speed. Despite this embarrassing moment, which still haunts me, of all Yorkshire's rivers, the Wharfe is still my favourite. I'm glad to have the chance to rediscover its gentle charm.

Dougie's Back

I met an old friend this week, who I hadn't seen for about two years. Dougie was not as pleased to see me as I was to see him again. He tilted his head to one side, opened his eyes wide and ruffled his gorgeous, green feathers. Dougie, of course, was a parrot, with whom we had the pleasure of making our first acquaintance five years ago, just after the start of filming for series two of *The Yorkshire Vet*.

He'd had a terrible time during a visit to a previous vet practice, where he had become so stressed and traumatised while having his beak and nails trimmed, that he had ended up spending the afternoon recovering in an oxygen tent. Margaret, his devoted owner/partner, did not want this to happen again, and came to see if I could help. With the benefit of experience from a veterinary nurse called Kate, we devised a way of enveloping the parrot's carrying cage in a plastic bag, enabling us to administer anaesthetic gas with the minimum of stress to the bird. Normally, of course, it is a very bad idea to put a living thing into a plastic bag, but under close supervision and with the provision of oxygen and anaesthetic gas, nothing could go wrong. We hoped.

On that day, everything went smoothly. Dougie was relaxed, although nobody else was, because the strength of avian-human bond between Dougie and Margaret was palpable and we could not bear to imagine the consequences of an anaesthetic accident.

And now he needed my help again. His beak and claws had grown again to a problematic length and the handsome, enigmatic and usually talkative parrot would require a GA to sort them out.

I found a suitably sized bag and recruited two helpers, one of which was Anne and both of whom happened to be slightly frightened of handling birds – especially a bad-tempered bird with a beak powerful enough to split the bulletproof casing of a walnut. But my assistants' reticence was not a hindrance. The joining of forces

and the pooling of energy and expertise is powerful. Luckily, powerful enough to overcome the fear of a big-beaked and slightly ferocious parrot. Soon Dougie's annoyed noises from within the bag ceased and, soon after, all parrot movement stopped. I peered inside. Dougie has succumbed completely and his head lolled backwards. I think he was snoring. I tore through the plastic and opened his cage. He was definitely under the effects of the gas and was fast asleep, but we didn't have long. Swift and combined action was required to scoop the flaccid bird out and into position to clip the elongated end of his beak and overgrown toes nails. Veterinary hearts were pumping quickly with anxiety for his health and recovery, with concern that he might wake up prematurely and either bite someone or escape, and with worry that his black nails might bleed if cut too short. I held him carefully and clipped his beak while Anne dealt with his nails and the task was completed in the nick of time.

Dougie's recovery was equally swift and he was back on his perch within minutes, with huge sighs of relief from all concerned. As he regained his composure, Anne and I watched the emerald beauty from a safe distance. He looked healthy but stupefied. Inside his travelling cage I spotted a child's music-making machine, with a big red button on the front. It was impossible to resist pressing the button, which resulted in a plinky-plonky tune similar to 'The wheels on the bus go round and round' emanating from the speaker.

We had to laugh as Dougie, the Amazonian Green with his beautiful plumage, actually started to dance on his perch.

It's Christmas!

At this time of year, more than any other, I am constantly amazed by the generosity of people. Grateful clients appear bearing gifts. Not gold, frankincense or myrrh, but bottles, chocolates and cards. This week, however, I had a more unusual gift – a framed oil painting, no less! Its subject, rather startlingly, was me. I was clutching a lamb and wore a maniacal smile. It was a good likeness of the lamb. Quirky as the oil painting was, it did have the obvious benefit of not adding to the girth of my waist – a perennial problem in December. The electronic dog scales in the waiting room get more use by staff than animals at this calorific time of the year!

Chris and Carol, with their Christmassy names, made their annual pre-Christmas visit for Sandy V to receive his vaccination. Sandy V is one of my favourite patients, because he was my very first appointment three years ago, when I started working in Boroughbridge. The "V", unlike the "V" in "Sputnik V", the Russian COVID vaccine (that stands for Vaccine), is like the "V" after a king – that is to say, "Sandy the Fifth". The stumpy Border terrier is the fifth in a long line of Borders owned by Chris and Carol. He was supremely healthy as usual. As they were leaving, Chris and Carol handed over a huge bag of festive gifts: some square and selection-box-shaped with my kids' names on, two bottle-shaped, one for the staff and

one for Anne and me, and one in the shape of a bone, labelled for Emmy. When I got home, and despite the protestations of my younger son Archie, who wanted his chocolate right away, I put the Norton presents under the Christmas tree, ready for the day itself.

We have seen a handful of dogs over the last couple of weeks who have shown a lack of self-restraint similar to Archie's where selection boxes under the Christmas tree are concerned. Chocolate is toxic to dogs, but luckily the actual amount of cocoa in most dairy-type chocolate is low, so disaster was averted in these cases. There are other challenges and dangers, too. I vividly remember, while at vet school, trying unsuccessfully to nurse a lurcher back to health after he had eaten a whole Christmas cake. Intravenous fluids, exploratory laparotomy and peritoneal lavage were all in vain. I think about that poor dog every time I see a greedy dog at Christmas.

The kitten who had started to vomit shortly after developing an interest in tinsel was another worry. Sparkly and cheerful as this festive decoration undoubtedly is, it is a very bad thing if ingested by a cat or dog. Tinsel definitely loses its appeal when it is surgically resected from mangled intestines. It happens quite frequently. I don't know why cats find it so tempting to swallow, but I wish they wouldn't.

Back at home, there was someone else struggling to exercise restraint in the face of festive excitement. Emmy, during a few hours left home alone one afternoon, had investigated under the tree. Much like Paddy the Jack Russell, the memorable dog of my childhood, who would savagely eviscerate every single chocolate-containing present, Emmy had sniffed out her gift from Sandy V. But she's a good girl. The patient dog had pulled it out into the middle of the room, but had not removed the wrapping paper. She, at least, had decided that she could wait until Christmas Day!

Lost Parakeet

"Call me Ishmael," I'm sure he whispered, as he sat on my shoulder. The brightly coloured parakeet was as talkative as he was lucky. It transpired that he was also very mischievous. He'd been brought into the practice just before Christmas in a box, having been found in a school playground. Within moments, there was a shriek from Tracy the practice manager. She loves dogs, clients and spreadsheets (in that order), but not birds. Ishmael, as I decided to call him after his whispered words, had escaped and was flying around the prep room. I rushed to the rescue but my first attempt to capture the colourful escapee failed. Eventually we managed to waft him into the isolation kennel and I pondered how best to get him back into his box. Luckily, the mini parrot liked to sit on shoulders and he came to me, rather than me going to him. His dulcet tones echoed in my ear. Was he *really* called Ishmael? Surely that name was synonymous with large whales rather than small parrots but, these days, anything is possible.

From his perch on my shoulder, it was fairly simple to pop him into the kennel.

The next plan involved a post on social media, which included a photo. It quickly spread exponentially and went viral at the same time and his owner, who was delighted that the escaped exotic bird had been found, soon came forward. We arranged for his collection later that day, after school. It turned out the micro-parrot was actually called Seb, not Ishmael as he had clearly told me earlier. His relieved owner recounted the story, as her son watched on, open-mouthed with excitement and happiness that he had been reunited with his friend:

"I'm so glad you've found him! He escaped this morning from the kitchen when I was taking the shopping from the car into the kitchen. Seb always likes to sit on a shoulder, even when I'm in the shower [I couldn't quite picture the scene]. Archie, my son – it's his bird really – has been worried all day."

There was another twist to the story, because Seb, as if in a children's story, had flown to Archie's school that morning.

"We didn't know how he knew the way, but he found it alright. The headmaster found him, sitting somewhere in the playground waiting for Archie to come out at break time," Archie's mum explained.

It was the headmaster who took time out of his busy day and brought Seb to us, although at that time, of course, he didn't know who the parakeet belonged to. Safely in the consulting room, I opened the temporary birdhouse/cat basket in which Seb was waiting. He popped out and immediately jumped onto Archie's shoulder. It was just like a scene from *Pirates of the Caribbean*. Seb started chatting excitedly to Archie, clearly delighted to be reunited with his best mate.

"Thank you for finding him," Archie said to me, with maturity beyond his seven years. "I have a feeling this won't be the last time you see him at your practice," he added. They were wise words with a crystal-clear foresight that many adults would be pleased to have. And, yes, we are all (well, maybe with the exception of Tracy) looking forward to Seb's next appearance at our practice, although hopefully it will be in less stressful circumstances – maybe a nail or beak trim? At least we know he'll be a model parakeet patient – talkative and very friendly. And at the end of a turbulent year, full of stress, fear, enforced isolation and anxiety, Seb's adventures cheered everyone up!

Seb, on the loose in the isolation kennels, looking for company.

A Potato!

Charlie the spaniel had been off it for a few days. Suffering from clinical signs of vomiting, loss of appetite and a sore abdomen, there were many things that could be the cause. Tests were required to find out what was going on. He'd had plenty of medication to help his pain, but the distended stomach, clearly visible on the radiograph, demanded immediate exploratory surgery.

An exploratory laparotomy – that is, an operation to look inside the abdomen – is often necessary to achieve a definitive diagnosis and effect an immediate cure and is always exciting. There is no substitute for actually seeing the contents of the abdomen, feeling along the intestines with your fingers and examining the liver and spleen in real life, rather than via the two-dimensional, grey and white shades of a scan or X-ray. And this proved to be exactly the case for Charlie.

There in front of us was the answer. In his duodenum, directly opposite the pancreas, there was a large ovoid object causing a complete blockage, explaining all the poor dog's signs. It was solid and smooth like a pebble, but had been invisible to the X-rays that had been taken the previous evening. Was it rubbery? Maybe. Anne, who was holding the scalpel, and I could only guess what it might be. Anne's sharp incision allowed the foreign body to bulge out through the intestinal wall, emerging like a new-born baby with a plop into my waiting fingers. Neither of us had seen anything like it before – well, we had, but not inside a dog.

"It's a POTATO," we exclaimed in unison, as the smooth, boiled spud appeared. In other circumstances, it would have looked delicious, but not now. By some potato miracle, it had been swallowed whole. The ovoid vegetable had avoided any form of digestion in the stomach and become stuck fast in the intestine. It reminded me of a similar incident, a couple of years ago. I had been treating a heifer, which had been grazing along the banks of the Swale all summer. The pneumonic signs from which she had been suffering had not improved with my injections and frothy fluid continued to emerge from her nose and mouth. She died the day after my visit and the farmer and I decided a post-mortem examination was required. When the report came back from the lab, several days later, I called the farmer with the unusual and unexpected diagnosis: a potato had been lodged in the lower part of the chest. The farmer was totally amazed at this revelation, exclaiming, just like Anne: "A POTATO?"

I confirmed the laboratory diagnosis and the vegetable.

"But we don't feed our cows on POTATOES," the farmer protested, emphasising the word potato just as forcefully.

"Well, apparently there was one stuck inside your heifer," I explained again.

"Wait a minute," came a more considered response after a short pause. "These cattle have been grazing along the river. There's a chance these potatoes [he didn't shout it so loudly this time] could have washed up in the flood water." It was definitely a possibility. Grazing beside a river prone to flooding is fraught with problems like this. He went on in a much more pragmatic tone, "I bet that's what's happened. Well, it's a relief because that's just one of those things, isn't it? Nothing else could have been done."

But back with Charlie, there was little chance he had swallowed a washed-up potato from the river, because this one was scrubbed and boiled. After the op, Anne and I drew straws to decide who would telephone the owner. I won and made the call. As I explained the unusual findings, two words came booming back down the telephone line:

"A POTATO?"

Dogs, Cats and Ferrets

It used to be simple. Of course it did. A cooperative system had evolved to facilitate a commonsense solution that made life easier. But that was then. Nowadays, devising a complicated, contrived and confusing solution seems to be all the rage.

I'm talking about the Pet Travel Scheme (RIP), which allowed the controlled and coordinated travel of dogs, cats and ferrets (yes, ferrets) on their holidays to continental Europe and a few other places. The concept and practice were straightforward, although the notion of a ferret enjoying a fortnight on the Costa del Sol was so abstract it could only be imagined as a surreal dream. However, the new post-Brexit reality of taking dogs, cats and ferrets to Europe is every bit as surreal as the prospect of a polecat, a pool and a pina colada.

Last week, as the UK ceased to be part of Europe, simplicity was replaced by something altogether different called an Animal Health Certificate, or AHC. We completed our first one this week. It took a mere two hours. The appropriate "gateway", where the required documents were hidden was as overgrown and difficult to negotiate as the side entrance to a derelict building, hidden from sight and tricky to get through. Once in, the list of links from which to choose was dizzying, with separate, bi-lingual documents in English and every other European language. For example, AHC07 covers *The Non-commercial Movement into a Member State from a Territory or Third Country* [that's us] *of Dogs, Cats or Ferrets – English/ Estonian.* There were twenty-two to choose from. We thanked our lucky stars that dogs, cats *and* ferrets had been bundled together on the same certificate. Otherwise, there might have been sixty-six to choose between. The practice's inaugural AHC was for a dog to go to Rotterdam, so AHC05 was selected. It was ten pages long, in both English and Dutch and was made up of text in a font so implausibly small that it necessitated either reading glasses or a magnifying glass, depending on the vet's age and ocular health; as much a test of eyesight as of the vet's certification skills.

I needed more help, so grabbed a large coffee and braced myself for a lengthy phone call to the export department at DEFRA. These phone calls are always time-consuming and usually slightly frustrating. The recent requirement to "work from home if you can", the festive hiatus in normal working hours and the alarm caused by the avian flu outbreak (which continues to spread below the radar, hidden by a more conspicuous virus) meant that my time waiting on hold was longer than usual. This was made more bearable because the recorded messages are by someone whose voice sounds very similar to Ringo Starr in his *Thomas the Tank Engine* days:

"Press one for Dog, Cat and Ferret travel to the EU; Press two for the Fat Controller's office," I kept expecting to hear. After more than half an hour on hold, my coffee had been consumed and I had to hang up without an answer. I trawled the official site a bit more and found some guidance notes that were clearer than those that came with the AHC05. By 11 a.m., the German shepherd had been checked and certified and was ready to head off on its holidays. The animal part of the convoluted scheme had been completed with some stress. For the owners though, more checks were required – a health check of their own in the form of a COVID test prior to travel. Amusingly, this had to happen in the scenic northern town of Barnard Castle. It was a necessary journey but in the wrong direction. I just hoped their eyesight was up to scratch!

Everybody Needs Good Neighbours

What should have been lunchtime turned into emergency surgery, following a phone call from the owners of a deerhound, who had been enjoying a snowy walk in the winter wonderland that was North Yorkshire. Willow had been running around, goodness knows exactly where or doing exactly what, but it must have been either at high speed or very close to the hind hooves of a bad-tempered horse, because she'd returned bedraggled with a painful and bloodied face. Maybe she'd slipped on the ice.

"I think she's broken her jaw," was the measured assessment from a calmer-than-expected owner. It turned out to be an accurate assessment, too. The crepitus was evident as I examined the injured hound and I explained that I would need to give her a general anaesthetic to allow a more detailed assessment and to take some X-rays. Once under GA, the fracture was clear. The radiographs showed that it ran obliquely through the horizontal part of the right jaw. There was a lot of wincing from nearby nurses, because there are not many sights more horrible nor sounds more grating than bone moving on bone. It was a nasty fracture but eminently fixable.

However, to do so I needed some specialist equipment. Luckily, our friends and neighbours at *Swift Referrals* were more than happy to lend me the required kit. This new and dynamic referral practice opened at almost exactly the same time as we did at Sandbeck, so we are both new kids on the block, so to speak; the next generation of independent practices. They are just around the corner at Thorpe Arch and their fantastic staff are always happy to help. We have

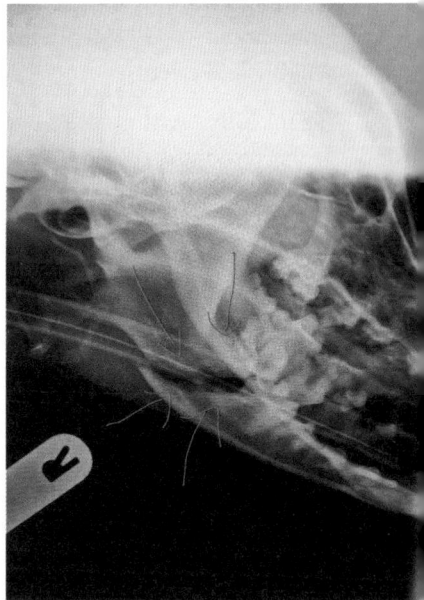

a great relationship – the sort that was commonplace among veterinary practices several decades ago, when all surgeries in an area helped each other out without a thought. Nights on call might be covered, in the event of illness or an important engagement and nobody would moan or complain if their extra shift resulted in a nocturnal call. I remember, many years ago, covering a Saturday night for a singlehanded practice in the neighbouring town. The practice owner had a family wedding to attend. I was on duty anyway and offered to cover any calls that might present themselves. "Oh, don't worry," reassured the vet as she packed her bags for a long overdue weekend away. "The practice is always quiet on a Saturday night." Even in the early days of my veterinary career I had enough experience to know that I should never believe that! I readied myself for a rammed weekend. And that was exactly what happened. First, a foaling – probably the most urgent and stress-inducing call on a vet's emergency list – at a distant stud, followed by a calf with a broken leg, shortly after midnight. But this didn't matter, because helping an injured animal was what it was all about and if we could help a neighbour too, then so much the better. In recent years, the dramatic changes in the profession – in part a result of the rash of corporate takeovers – have meant that the historic warm, friendly and symbiotic relationship that was once taken for granted has changed to protectionism over long-established clients.

Thankfully, within the veterinary world, things seem gradually to be moving back towards a more cooperative way of working. Thanks to our new and special relationship with our neighbour, I was quickly on the case, repairing Willow's broken jaw. The jagged edges met perfectly and soon normal stability was restored. Plenty of painkillers and a numbing nerve block later, Willow was groggy but awake, wondering what had just happened. I called her owners, who had been on tenterhooks, with the good news. The fragments of her fractured jaw had been happily and perfectly reunited and normality was restored.

Livestock-Guarding Dogs and
Save the Cheetah, Save the World

I met a laidback and very handsome chap this week. His name was Arthur. A veterinary surgery in Wetherby was just not interesting enough and he lounged, half asleep on the consulting room floor. His name seemed to suit him. He looked like a lazy golden retriever but his owner, indignant at my incorrect identification of this unusual breed, put me right.

"He's not a golden retriever – that's what everyone thinks. He's actually a Maremma. He's a livestock-guarding dog." His owner was clearly passionate about this breed, its provenance and heritage. It turned out that Arthur's ancestors hailed from the mountains of Italy, where they had the important role of guarding flocks of sheep from wolves and other predators. Arthur's forefathers would lounge around all day, just like he was doing in my consulting room, but would spring into action if anyone or anything came to threaten the safety of the animals under their care. It was a fascinating story and a role that I had not considered before. Of course, in England, where predators such as wolves do not exist, dogs help farmers by rounding up sheep or cows, when they need to be gathered from the fells or moved to new grazing. The breeds that have evolved are those that are nimble and quick, and have an innate ability to herd. But in southern and eastern Europe, the role of these guard dogs, which blend in with the flock of sheep or herd of goats, has been crucial. Over tea that evening, I regaled the story of this fascinating historical animal interrelationship.

After an evening Zoom meeting later that same week, with a brilliant organisation called the Cheetah Conservation Fund (CCF), it became evident that using dogs to guard livestock is very much an activity of the present, if not the future.

Cheetahs are in trouble. There are only 7,000 left in the wild and they are on the cusp of becoming endangered. One of the causes of this is persecution by impoverished farmers as they – entirely understandably – try to protect their precious sheep and goats from predation by this, the slightest and most unassuming of the big cats. This is where the modern livestock-guarding dog comes into play. In Namibia, they are using Anatolian shepherd dogs. Originally, these dogs protected Turkish goats from wolves and bears, but nowadays their presence deters hungry cheetahs from roaming too close to the farmers' rifles. As I learnt all about this amazing utilitarian relationship between man and animal, I promised I would try to help raise awareness of this wonderful animal altruism. The dogs stay with their flock or herd and become a full-time member of the gang, forming a bond that will last not just a lifetime, but through many generations. Pups imprint from as early as a few weeks of age, mainly by olfactory stimuli, although full training takes as long as two years. A good livestock-guarding dog must have, just like anyone, the key attributes of trustworthiness, attentiveness and protectiveness. It's no good if they lose interest and wander off. The CCF started this Livestock Guarding programme in 1994 and it has been hugely successful, reducing the cheetah losses by more than 80%. So, obviously not many dogs have wandered off!

My interest was piqued and I investigated more examples of this phenomenon. I'd heard about alpacas protecting newborn lambs from the dangers of foxes, but then I found a canine helper closer to home. There's a chicken farm in West Yorkshire which uses guarding dogs to keep predators at bay! Livestock guarding, it turns out, is alive and well!

More information on cheetah conservation can be found at www. cheetah.org

The Dog with Two Brains

Amber's owners assured me that there was absolutely no chance that she could have eaten anything unusual. Her relaxed demeanour and her relaxed abdomen left me equally relaxed to begin with, even though for a six-month-old pup who had vomited umpteen times over the last few days a foreign body was high on the list of possible causes.

There are a multitude of conditions that make dogs vomit, ranging from simple gastritis, via pancreatitis to serious organ disease. Somewhere in the middle of the spectrum of seriousness lies the presence of an obstructing foreign body. Vets use all their powers of deduction to work out if this is a possibility. First, we take a detailed history. The cat that had swallowed a condom, for example, came with a very definite (and rather embarrassing) story, and said foreign body was therefore quickly found and removed. The false teeth, on the other hand, came with a vague history that they only *might* have been swallowed, which resulted in a long, and ultimately fruitless (or toothless) search.

Examination by abdominal palpation is next. The fingers of an experienced physician can be many times more sensitive than a radiograph. Round rubber balls, for example, are particularly easy to palpate. A partially digested corn-on-the-cob, stolen from a barbecue and lodged in the small intestine also has a distinctive shape and bumpy surface. But other things – socks, plastic bags, or even partially chewed party poppers – are not so easy to feel. X-rays can come to the rescue, but not always. Whilst the arms, legs and ears of a Mickey Mouse stuffed toy can show up clearly

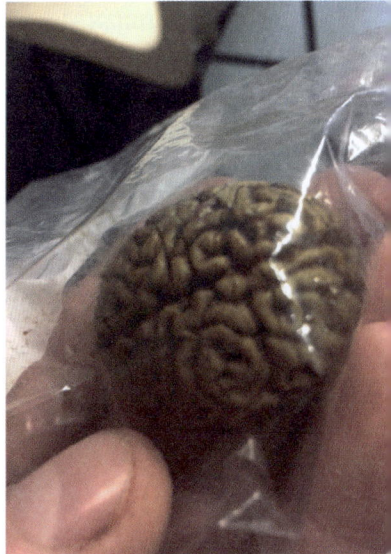

and amusingly in shades of grey, many foreign bodies are invisible to X-rays, disguised as normal abdominal contents. Other clues on an X-ray can help though. Abnormal gas patterns suggest an object is obstructing normal passage through the bowel. And this was the case with Amber. Plans were made to take her to theatre.

What we found in Amber, despite earlier assertions to the contrary, was indeed a foreign body. It was soft, which made it impossible to palpate, and made of rubbery plastic, which made it invisible to X-rays. Lodged firmly in the intestines, the peculiar structure had done well to squeeze itself out of the stomach. It plopped/bounced into a kidney dish, almost ending up on the floor. What on earth was it? It was too flat to be a ball. Its surface was crisscrossed with sulci and gyri. There was a cerebellum in its hindquarters and was that also a medulla? Without doubt, the object that had just been removed from Amber's intestines was a tiny brain. It was prodded with instruments. Surely an actual brain, from a rodent or mole or rabbit, would have been chewed, mangled and digested past the point of causing an obstruction? Prodding proved it to be made of a rubbery material, presumably from a model, (although who has a scale model of a human brain in their house, waiting for an inquisitive puppy to eat, we all wondered?).

The rest of the surgery went fine and Amber was soon as good as new. By morning, she was wagging her tail just like beforehand, but with just one brain in her body. The lively, young Labrador had been dubbed (by me) *The Dog with Two Brains*, none too subtly referencing one of the funniest films of all time, featuring the genius Steve Martin. If you've not watched this film, you should. It contains one of the most hilarious lines of all time. And, when you've watched it, you'll never see those acid soil-loving plants called azaleas again, without raising a smile or laughing out loud.

Joining Forces

Castrating a donkey is not the same as gelding a pony. For various reasons, it requires closer attention to detail. The anaesthetic is not quite as simple as it would be in a horse and the existence of extra blood vessels down there demands ligation as well as the usual clamping action with a special tool called an emasculator. So, when I got a message from a client who needed help with her donkey, it was not exactly the proverbial, and now literal, pain in the ass; but I did need a second pair of hands.

Luckily, I have a partner in crime – or at least an accomplice in all things donkey – and I was quick to send him a message. It wasn't quite an SOS, but I was pleased when Matt offered an immediate and affirmative response. Matt is a vet from the heart of West Yorkshire, with whom I've worked on a few occasions. The first was during an early episode of *Springtime on the Farm*, when we were both "expert presenters". We chuckled about this moniker all afternoon, because neither of us fitted either part of the description. The next time we worked together was when I needed help with a donkey called Gary. He had a growth on his penis that needed to be removed under GA. Matt, whose practice was close by, was happy to lend a hand. The procedure, which could have been very stressful, went smoothly with Matt's calm and competent assistance at the anaesthetic end. He was full of the natural enthusiasm of youth and I really enjoyed working with him. He was the natural choice for an assistant for another donkey event.

We arrived at more or less the same time and I was delighted to see that Matt had brought a huge selection of extra kit, packed into a capacious fishing box. No piece of equipment had been left behind (except for the fishing tackle) and no eventuality would see us short of drugs or instruments. We had to decide which of us would do the surgery and who would do the anaesthetic. The historical hierarchy of vets dictates that the more senior vet does the cutting while the junior one ensures the patient stays asleep.

Over my career, I've been the junior on too many occasions, with the almost-always-challenging job of sedating a boisterous/wild yearling and maintaining anaesthesia for the duration of the procedure. It is always more stressful and more prone to problems than the role of the surgeon. Today, with my hair thinning and greying at an alarming rate, seemed the perfect time to pull rank. We pondered doses and drug combinations and junior Matt drew up the appropriate combinations into syringes of various sizes and aimed for the jugular. Before we knew it, the donkey was asleep and the surgery was done. It couldn't have gone more perfectly.

Clearly impressed at the efficiency of our new partnership, the donkey's canny owner had another idea.

"We have this colt over here, too. I've been meaning to get him gelded for a while. You don't fancy doing him as well while you're here, do you, lads?' He gestured to a loose box across the yard. Like Batman and Robin, we couldn't turn down another challenge and went to have a look over the table door. Inside, was a strong and stocky coloured cob, who immediately swung his back end in my direction and kicked the inside of the stable door so hard that it must have dented the wood.

"There you go, Julian," said Matt as he handed the bottles and syringes over with a large grin. "It's your turn to do the sedation."

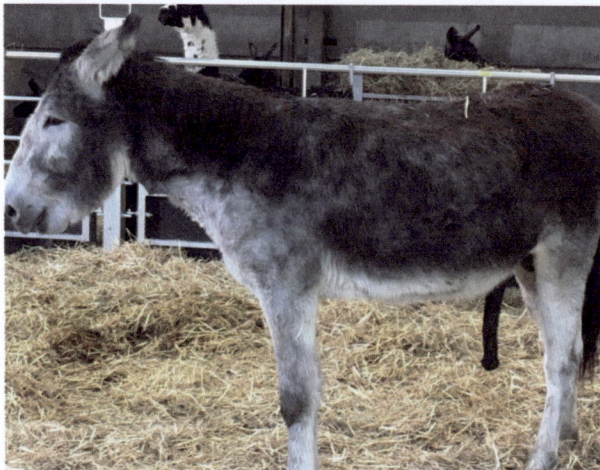

Gary, a former patient, treated by Matt and me.

Duck, Not Running

The runner duck was obviously not right. He couldn't even walk, let alone run. It was even a struggle for the young duck to hold his head upright. The presence of Mo (named after the world-famous long-distance runner) on the appointment list might have caused a degree of panic from some vets, sending them running to search the internet. Lame ducks, a bit like damp squibs, could be managed. Limp ones were a completely different kettle of fish. As it happened, and according to the owners, Professor Google suggested the requirement for worming treatment, but I have a healthy suspicion of any computer-generated diagnosis either via generic websites or ill-constructed algorithms. Besides, I've treated plenty of birds before and I did not need either of these things.

Like his namesake, Mo was slender, but that's where the similarity stopped. His legs were floppy and weak, as was his neck. Standing up was difficult. When I held him and gently lowered his body so that his webbed feet rested on the table I met with no resistance. Everything stayed floppy. Mo had no go. He'd lost his mojo.

I asked some questions about his siblings, all of which were fine. Then, I attempted a neurological examination. This is not something I'm very good at. Neurology should be simple, but it isn't. At least, it isn't to me. Whilst I know about nerves, where they go, what they do, how they might go wrong and what to do about it, the subject has never been my forte. Cardiology, ophthalmology, internal medicine, dermatology, obstetrics – all got me top marks. But not neurology. I've tried to get better, attending courses when such things were allowed. But I'm always distinctly average. However, my limited neurology knowledge was sufficient to diagnosis Mo's problem.

The little duck was suffering from botulism.

Botulism is a nasty disease, caused by the toxin produced by the bacterium Clostridium botulinum. The toxin causes neuromuscular paralysis of pretty much any or all of the muscles in the body, depending on the dose ingested. When injected into a wrinkled, saggy face or a furrowed brow at a beautician's parlour, botulinum toxin leaves the muscles paralysed, rendering the overlying skin completely smooth, a bit like the effects of a good plasterer. If it gets into a duck or a cow (the two instances where vets usually encounter the toxin), the result is usually death. Ducks seem particularly prone, as they ingest the ubiquitous bacteria in muddy ponds or puddles. It's an occupational hazard if you're a duck and impossible to avoid. Luckily, it's only a very sporadic condition.

If cattle get it, the results can be devastating. Accidental ingestion – usually via contaminated silage or inadvertently eating dead rodents – leads to the toxin being absorbed and problems ranging from acute death to a slow, lingering one. Affected cattle lie around, as if dazed and dopey, not eating, drinking or moving. It's hard to diagnose and usually requires an experienced vet who has seen it before, rather than expensive tests, all of which come back with negative results. I once saw a case of heifers which had been exposed to botulism when the half-eaten bones of dead poultry, dropped in the field by a fox, contaminated their parched and bare pasture. Finding this final clue in the jigsaw took several weeks.

But back to Mo. In severe cases, treatment is futile. The toxin has wreaked its damage by the time the clinical picture appears. But mild cases can improve, with supportive treatment and doses of penicillin to kill any of the incriminating bacteria. I talked through the options and we decided to give it a go.

The next day, Mo was back. Miraculously, he was improving. His neck was more sturdy and his legs more robust. I drew up a second dose. Maybe Mo's running days were not over just yet?

The Highland Vet

I'm not sure if this is a coincidence, but the practice where my veterinary career began is also now on television, in the middle of its first series on Channel 5. The programme is called *The Highland Vet* and follows the animal adventures of farmers, pet owners and veterinary surgeons in Thurso, in the very north of Scotland. Thurso is a bleak but beautiful part of the world and I am reminded of the time I spent there whenever I see the trailers or the promotional posts on social media for this new series.

Veterinary students need to spend many weeks during the university holidays "seeing practice" with a vet, in order to learn crucial practical skills. As an energetic vet student, my plan was always to find the best, busiest and most enthusiastic practices in which to do this. If that practice happened to be two days' drive north of Yorkshire, then so be it. I'd learnt a lot at busy vets in York, Skipton and Wetherby and I had spent weeks in Gloucestershire following cattle vets around and watching them insert their gloved arm inside hundreds of cows. I'd even flown to Philadelphia Vet School to embark on an externship in the veterinary ER. Had I accepted the job offered to me at the end of my tenure there, my life would have been very different.

But I didn't and, having made that decision, a career based in the UK beckoned. After my final student placement at McGregor and Partners, Thurso, I was offered a temporary job, to cover the tail-end of the calving season and to help with holiday cover. Of course, despite its huge distance from friends and family, I accepted without hesitation because this was an excellent place to cut my veterinary teeth and a wonderful part of the world to explore for a few months. It was definitely more down to earth than the alternative opportunity on the other side of the Atlantic.

In a wild and beautiful place, my learning curve was as exponential as the use of this word recently. Hungrily, I gathered new skills and soaked up experience and knowledge like an absorbent sponge. I made mistakes and had some near misses, some of which still give me nightmares. Others I've managed to expunge. The first, memorable mistake I made could easily have been unmemorable, because it left me confused and concussed with a temporarily damaged brain. The well-aimed kick from the left hind foot of a cow so wild that she could only be captured by lasso, left me reeling, dazed and upside down in a dirty pile of straw. I'd optimistically attempted to take a sample of peritoneal fluid from this apparently poorly cow. The patient had only recently experienced human beings, as she had spent almost all her life roaming the rough fells of Caithness. In retrospect, introducing a long and wide-bore needle into her abdominal cavity, however carefully I tried to do so, was a crazy idea. Moments later, the stars spinning in front of my eyes confirmed it had been a bad decision. The throbbing head and blurred vision lasted for several days and even put me off imbibing whisky at the weekend ceilidh. Indeed, the very fact I was at a ceilidh at all was a sign that my cognitive process was severely traumatised – I usually avoid organised dancing like the plague!

Fortunately, I recovered uneventfully and threw myself back into the life and culture of Caithness, having learnt a healthy regard for the fast-moving feet of bad-tempered Caithness cattle. My recollections and memories of that unique place are too many to be described here, although another time I might regale readers with the story of the case that I thought signalled the end my veterinary career when it had only just begun...

Goats and Halloumi

It was a very early start, but there was a lot to get through. The night before I had scrutinised the schedule and the miles I'd need to cover. It reminded me how huge Yorkshire really is and the five o'clock alarm was crucial if I was to get everywhere on time. My tasks would, once again, take me out of my normal comfort zone. I'd had a phone call a few weeks previously from a friend, who happens to be the series producer of a popular TV programme about farming. Despite everything, including the necessity for an early wake-up call, I knew my arm would be twisted to help. I also knew it would be an exciting and interesting day, learning new skills and meeting people passionate about their work; both these things are good.

My role was surrounded by large inverted commas, because I was described as the "expert presenter". Of course, in reality I was neither of these things. I'm a vet and not an expert on either presenting or the task in hand today, which was to make cheese. I'm definitely a fan of cheese, but I wouldn't go as far as to say I was an expert. But before the cheese, we needed milk and I do know a bit about this. Off I set, in horrible sleet and snow, to the far side of Skipton where I was to meet Sharon and her herd of goats. It was a dark and bleak journey, with sufficient cars upside down

in ditches or crashed into stonewalls to keep me focused on the road at a sensibly low speed.

Eventually, I arrived and we set about milking the goats. Yield was low because most of the herd were in the final stages of pregnancy, but after about an hour I had a large plastic barrel filled past halfway with creamy goats' milk. It looked so velvety and sumptuous I could not resist taking out half a glass to drink. It tasted as delicious as it looked. I strapped the plastic barrel into the passenger seat of my car and headed into deepest, darkest West Yorkshire where the goats' milk would be transmogrified into Halloumi cheese.

On one of the snowiest days of the year, the satnav of my trusty Subaru must have fancied giving the car and me another challenge as it delighted in sending me up and down the steepest and narrowest of minor roads. It was a beautiful drive, but the 4x4 capability was tested. Halfway along the journey my phone rang. It was a production assistant who told me the camera crew, who were trying to follow, had re-routed via the M62 and might be delayed. All the time, the milk was sploshing and splashing around inside its barrel. I feared it would turn into butter rather than cheese.

Finally, the milk, the film crew and I were all in the same place – Sowerby Bridge – and the process of cheese-making began. Razan was in charge. This inspirational lady and her family arrived in Yorkshire as refugees from the war in Syria. With a pharmacy degree, but without a job, she turned her hand to making the finest quality Halloumi cheese – Yorkshire Squeaky Cheese. Today, I would be making my own. Almost like a magic potion, a small dose of a brown liquid called rennet started the process. The enzymes, once naturally derived from the stomach of a ruminant but now synthetic and vegetarian-friendly, curdled the casein, forming solid lumps. After forty-five minutes the lumps were removed and squashed into blocks. Once the excess liquid had been drained off, the blocks were boiled in the remnants of the liquid whey. Hey presto! I'd made cheese!

Foot and Mouth

Twenty years ago tomorrow (7 March 2001) was a bad day. It marked the first case of Foot and Mouth Disease to be discovered in Yorkshire. The affected farm was in the heart of Wensleydale and it will not claim any fame – it was the tip of an iceberg as significant as any that have caused nautical accidents.

If there was to be a league table of viruses, in terms of infectivity, Foot and Mouth Disease Virus (FMDV) would be at the top of the premier division. Within a herd of cows, in less than a day all of the animals would be standing still, subdued and salivating. On closer examination, the inside of every animal's mouth would be ulcerated to such an extent that the whole surface of the tongue would slough off. Granted, despite morbidity rates of 100% (that is to say, *all* animals would be sick; there was no such thing as an asymptomatic individual) the mortality rates were relatively low. At least, they would have been low had the affected cattle, sheep and pigs not been rounded up and shot in the head. With certainty, the slaughter squads guaranteed a 100% death rate.

The effects on the rural community cannot be overstated. Herds and flocks built up over generations were wiped out. Movement restrictions caused welfare nightmares. Disinfection points were constructed along farm tracks and rural lanes, more in hope than expectation that the disease could be held back. In the days before smartphones, reliable emails and the accurate dissemination of data, rumour and gossip were the main source of information about *Infected Premises* as they were dramatically dubbed. The sight of groups of strangers, clad from head to toe in white sent fear across a region. When a local bowling club met in a layby, to share a lift to York for an away game, passers-by panicked, thinking they were vets from the Ministry, all wearing protective suits. Thankfully that new case turned out to be a false alarm.

But there were sufficient non-false alarms to ruin everything. The first case I came across was early one Thursday morning. I was on duty at Thirsk Auction Mart, checking cattle and sheep for suspicious lesions. I'd been there since 5 a.m. Despite having been checking cattle on a beef unit until well after dark the previous evening, my adrenaline level was sufficient to keep me awake and focused. I was also on call for normal veterinary emergencies. My phone rang; it was a farmer and I could hear the concern in his voice.

"I'm worried, Julian. I have a field of heifers. Bert and I checked them this morning and they look awful. Salivating and not moving." My heart sank. It was the first case of FMDV directly to affect a farm within the practice and I knew it would be a hammer blow to everyone in and around Thirsk. I called the Ministry and left them to it.

If we are honest, veterinary profession struggled. The leadership from above was woeful. Some vets, in the absence of routine work, helped with the surveillance checks. One vet I know travelled from North Yorkshire to Leeds each morning to receive instructions on which farms to visit, only to retrace his tracks up the A1, travelling for an extra three hours each hectic day. Movement licences arrived via the over-worked fax machine, if we were lucky. Later, at the end of the day, the photocopier strained under equal pressure. Staff and farmers were just as stressed, as rules changed on a daily basis. The OS map pinned to the wall of the office had more circles of infectivity every day. Each day, another client lost their stock and the future of the practice, into which I had just bought as a junior partner, appeared to be ebbing away like sand through an hourglass.

Recollections of Past Pleasures

My journey on snowy roads to the goat farm on the far side of Skipton demanded my full attention. It also evoked memories of my first foray into the world of farm animal veterinary practice. Brought up in industrial Castleford, my efforts to gather sufficient experience to have any chance of gaining a place at vet school needed a boost. Luckily, my schoolmate and fellow budding vet, Mark, and I found ourselves a lambing job with lodgings in a caravan, on a sheep farm in the middle of the district of Craven.

We'd alternate our work – Mark would spend a day at the veterinary practice in nearby Skipton, while I worked on the farm, breaking the ice on water troughs and learning about lambing. The next day we'd swap. I can remember my first vet day in detail. As it was before I could drive, it was either a bus journey or a cold, six-mile, death-defying cycle ride to the surgery. It was death-defying because of the juggernauts carrying stone from a nearby quarry and it was cold because this was the tail-end of winter and snow was in the air. Of course, to save fifty pence, I opted for the bike and I arrived for my first day with a farm vet bedraggled, shivering and splattered with mud. I thrust out a hand to the round, red-faced, tweed-clad vet who ran the practice. His name was Norman.

"My word, you've got cold hands," were his introductory words,

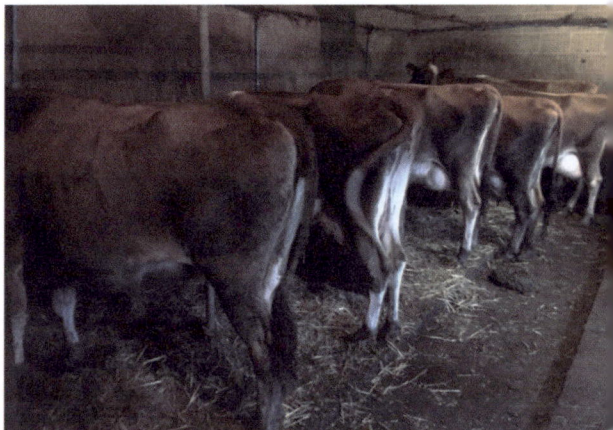

Cows in a byre. A common sight, even twenty-five years ago. Not so much nowadays!

quickly followed by, "Grab your wellies and coat, we've got some cows to see."

The first farm we visited was straight out of a Herriot book, with simple stone buildings clinging to a hillside. The farmer appeared as soon as we arrived, his thin, rugged face peering from under a battered flat cap. Norman handed me a box of equipment and fastened his long, brown, cotton coat, which made him look like a school caretaker. I struggled to keep up as the senior vet strode along at breakneck pace. Years later, once qualified, I realised that fast walking is an important trait for busy practising vets: there is usually a lot to do. It's also a good way to keep warm. I followed Norman and the farmer into a cow byre where a dozen brown cows were standing next to each other patiently chewing their cud or munching silage. It was the first time I'd been inside a building like this and I found it fascinating. It was surprisingly warm inside and the cows were surrounded by piles of deep straw. The warm air had a sweet smell, with both the fragrant odour of aromatic esters from the silage and the various smells from the cows themselves. The animals belched, passed faeces and urinated with such frequency that their biological habits seemed to be a full-time job.

Without any explanation, Norman donned a long, plastic glove and inserted his arm directly into the rectum of the nearest cow. *What on earth is he doing?* I wondered, never having witnessed anything like this before. He was in right up to his shoulder.

"No, I'm sorry, she's not," Norman said to the farmer, shaking his head. The farmer put a cross next to the cow's name in his notebook. "She has a cyst on her left ovary," Norman added, before repeating the same process with the next cow along. I was amazed that neither cow seemed to mind the internal examination. Eventually, I plucked up courage to ask what he was doing with his right arm, so deeply inside the patient.

"I'm feeling her uterus and ovaries. I can tell if she is pregnant or not." To a wide-eyed, naive schoolboy this seemed like magic; and from that moment, I was hooked.

Podcast Season

Until fairly recently, the phenomenon of the podcast was something of which I was only vaguely aware. However, just over a year ago, when meeting people in person or having a social gathering was still perfectly acceptable, my friend and collaborator Kate Fox suggested we record some of our theatre shows to turn them into podcasts under the racy title of *The Naked Vet*. It was meant to be a funny name, with half a nod towards Jamie Oliver's first cooking series and the other half of the nod to the occasions when I've removed layers of clothing to make a veterinary farm job more hygienic. And the audio format removed any scope for objectification, which was also good. But, like many things last year, they have ground to a halt. Instead, I've found myself as the guest in various virtual podcasts rather than the host, which has been a more comfortable place to be.

Continuing the naked theme, I was invited to join Kat and Jen, two stars from BBC Radio Sheffield. Their famously – or maybe infamously – candid podcasts are *actually* recorded naked, which initially seemed to be much *less* comfortable. Obviously, this was unusual and weird, but accurate angling of the laptop and precise positioning of the table allowed the maintenance of some degree of modesty. Our hour-long chat was very funny and, by the end, it felt completely normal to be chatting to two strangers without clothes.

My next event was slightly warmer. I was chatting to the first and only Dame I have ever met. The lady in question was Dame Evelyn Glennie. Once again, in advance, I made sure my collection of Mr Men and Little Miss books were prominently arranged as a backdrop to our Zoom meeting. But this turned out to be totally irrelevant, because our chat kept me totally absorbed. Dame Evelyn is regarded as one of the world's leading percussionists. It is impossible to do her justice in this short piece – the list of her achievements is almost endless. What makes Evelyn's success even more remarkable is that she is profoundly deaf and has described how she has honed her awareness of sound to such an extent that she considers her body to be a "resonating chamber". We covered lots of topics, including the importance of proper listening. I concurred and reflected upon the importance of this as a diagnostician, where listening to the owner's description of a problem, as well as using our other senses to the full, is crucial. Watching a patient, touching and palpating can provide much of the information we need, before ever reaching for a blood tube or ultrasound scanner.

I've also recorded another exciting podcast for Medic Mentor. They are the UK's largest medical social enterprise and their aim is to widen access to medicine and veterinary medicine by providing information, courses and resources for potential medical and veterinary school applicants. I was asked by a couple of vet students to help, by providing an accurate insight into the life of a veterinary surgeon. The veterinary medicine course is long, hard and expensive. The job, at the other end, is incredibly rewarding, but can also be challenging, often stressful and is typically poorly paid, so it is essential that potential students are fully aware of the downs as well as the ups of this amazing profession at an early stage. There were no rose-tinted spectacles, but an accurate guide to potential candidates about ways to enhance their chances of gaining a coveted place at vet school. It's a great idea and I was glad to help because, as every sensible person knows, young people are the future. It's the responsibility of us all to help and encourage the next generation.

Saturday Morning Caesarean

Saturday mornings can be an excellent time to do an emergency caesarean. Fortified by coffee and breakfast, no life-or-death challenge is too large.

Of course, it isn't always excellent. Many years ago, at the start of my veterinary career, I rushed up Sutton Bank, through the clouds, to perform a caesarean section on a young heifer. The isolated barn was just visible in the distance as I turned off the road near Hawnby. The usual wonderful view stretching north towards Snilesworth Moor was not visible at all. Thick fog obscured one of my favourite Yorkshire vistas. But my task on that Saturday was crystal clear. The enormous feet, crossed and immoveable, protruding from the back end of the exhausted heifer lying in the straw, told me everything I needed to know. Usually, a vet would call the surgery for the assistance of a colleague, to provide a second pair of hands to pass things, lift the calf and hold up the incised uterus for suturing at the end of the procedure. But I could picture the waiting room back at the practice, already bursting with anxious owners and their pets. Saturday morning open surgeries could be chaotically busy, often with twenty or thirty animals arriving almost simultaneously. It was full-on with three vets working and now, in my absence, they'd be down to two. To call for more help cow-side would leave a single

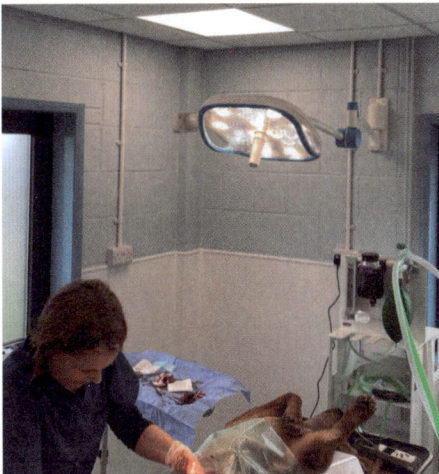

vet, stressed and drowning under clinical notes. So, I decided to crack on alone and hoped for the best. In fact, all went well, and I even got back in time to help clear the backlog of cats in the waiting room at the end of surgery.

By comparison, last Saturday proved to be the perfect time to deliver babies into the world. The basset hound was not progressing with normal labour and it was clear that a caesarean was required. What was less clear, however, was how our new surgery would cope. It was the first day that our new practice in Thirsk was operational, so the procedure would be as much a test of our new kit as it was a clinical challenge. Anne and I admitted the enormous hound, whose bulging abdomen was almost touching the ground. Lindsay and India, our fabulous nurses, had organised all the shiny new equipment in the new cupboards, but we now had to find what we needed (and any veterinary nurse will tell you that there is such a thing as a "vet-look" which means we search for ages for something that is right in front of us).

After a few minutes of searching, we'd found the anaesthetic, the syringes and needles. We'd also found the surgical kits and sutures and everything else we required. Anne hugged the pregnant patient as I drew a deep breath and injected the first drug ever to be used at Thirsk Veterinary Centre. From here, it didn't matter where the surgical suite was situated or that this was the first operation in our new business. I made the incision and before long, eight baby bassets were squeaking and searching for milk. It had been a very successful Saturday morning surgery and augured well for the future. We handed the basket full of puppies over to the proud owner. It had been an emotional first experience for us all. For the litter of healthy, hungry bassets, and for the future of Thirsk Veterinary Centre, everything looked rosy! Clinical task complete, we headed back to the prep room. A caesarean on any species is messy and Anne exclaimed in horror as we inspected the mess: "My lovely new theatre!" Splattered in blood, mucous and fluids of various shades, the next task involved cloths, mops and buckets.

Nobody Puts Baby in the Corner

Baby had a very sore eye. It was the result of an incident with an over-enthusiastic puppy whilst playing on a walk and the painful ulcer was stubbornly refusing to heal. This is a common problem in all corneal ulcers, but especially in dogs with round and bulging eyes. Being a French bulldog, Baby's eyes were bulgier than most. The central portion of the cornea – the surface of the eyeball – is most vulnerable to injury, on account of its extra protrusion and that same bulbous exposure means healing is often poor. The see-through surface of the eye is bereft of blood vessels, to allow light to pass through to the lens and then to the retina. In other areas of the body, blood vessels provide the elixir for repair, so on the cornea, a scratch or ulcer is up against it when compared to an ulcer on the tongue or a nick in the skin.

In order to get Baby's ulcer to heal I needed to carry out a fiddly procedure called a *grid keratectomy*, whereby the dead surface cells of the eye ulcer are debrided back to healthy corneal tissue by scraping the lesion with a hypodermic needle. It sounds horrendous but, done under full general anaesthetic, it works very well to kick start the recovery process. I explained my proposal to Baby's owner, who trusted my plan. Sometimes, the notion seems so counterintuitive that the description of the procedure evokes revulsion from a worried owner: "You're going to scratch the surface of my dog's eye with a needle? And you expect that will *help*?"

I took her through to prep, where I introduced her to the assembled collection of nurses. I absolutely love the 1980s film *Dirty Dancing*. It's soppy, I know, but we are all allowed guilty pleasures and I couldn't resist levering in the obvious joke.

"This is Baby. She has a corneal ulcer, which I need to fix. The question is, where can we put her?" I asked.

"Kennels four and five are free. So is the walk-in one, although that will be too big for her," Lucy the head nurse explained.

"I can't put her in there," I exclaimed, "because remember: *Nobody puts Baby in the corner*!" I had started chuckling to myself before I'd even finished my hilarious sentence, but blank faces stared back at me, obviously unaware of the classic scene. Needless to say, I repeated the same joke multiple times to everyone else in the building, before finally fastening Baby securely to the dog park in the centre of our prep room whilst her sedative took effect. She sat there, happily greeting everyone who passed by her. Her stumpy tail tried to wag, but the result was more of a body wag than a tail wag. The surgery went to plan and all the rough and irregular edges of the corneal lesion were swiftly sorted out. Nature would have a better chance of doing its thing now that the dead tissue was removed. But I had one final trick up my sleeve, to give nature another helping hand. I took a large syringe of blood from her jugular vein and set it to spin in the centrifuge to separate the red cells from the plasma. Plasma is jam-packed with proteins and healing factors and, when applied directly to the eye like biological eye-drop, accelerates repair. Armed with multiple little syringes of this plasma I took the happy little dog out to be reunited with her owner. If she could have talked, I'm sure she'd have explained that she'd "had the time of her life..." – you'll have to watch *Dirty Dancing* if you don't know what I'm talking about!

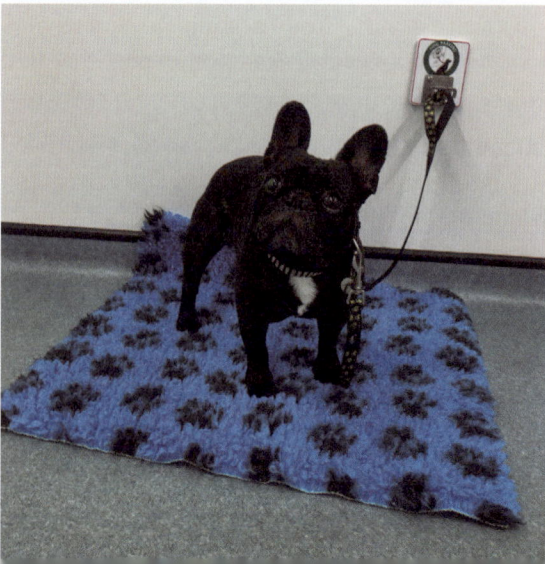

Swelling on the Leg and Geoffrey the Goat

The second opinion on Friday morning filled me with dread, even from the far side of the waiting room. It wasn't the loud barking emanating from behind nervous, saliva-splattered canine teeth that worried me. Rather, it was the localised swelling just above the carpal joint on the left front leg of the young German shepherd cross. I'd seen similar things many times before and I suspected the necessary X-rays would not yield good news.

The previous vets, struggling as we all have been with COVID restrictions, had opted for a hands-off "let's monitor this firm, painful swelling" approach, which had, unfortunately, failed to take into account that this was a prime predilection sight for a horrible tumour called an osteosarcoma. I examined the lump, and then warned about the possibility of a grave prognosis, before taking the (now friendly) fluffy dog off to have said X-rays. The first time I saw an osteosarcoma was in an Irish setter I was looking after at vet school, some twenty-odd years ago. That day, the diagnosis, radiographic images and subsequent treatments were etched, indelibly, onto my veterinary brain, never to be forgotten.

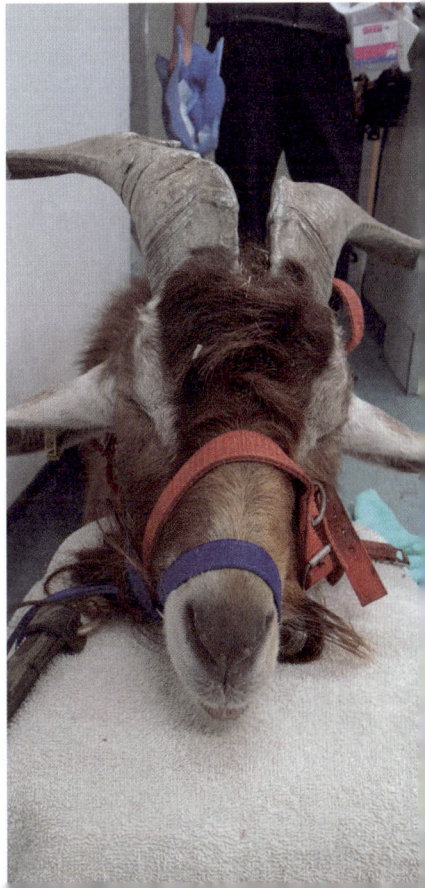

Sure enough, today's radiographs confirmed my suspicions and more serious discussions were required about the way ahead. Limb amputation followed by a course of chemotherapy would offer the best chance of survival, but it was a lot for the owners to take in when they'd been led to believe the problem was simply a strain.

Later, the gloomy mood was lifted by the arrival of Geoffrey. This happens a lot in the topsy-turvy world of veterinary practice. Sad cases are swiftly balanced out by happier patients, which always seem to appear at the opportune moment. Geoffrey was a fully-grown billy-goat, rehomed because of his over-amorous tendencies and now requiring castration before going to the new farm. It fell to me to perform the honours. For some reason, in my mind's eye, I had imagined that Geoffrey was a small goat, easy to carry into the vets. In reality, he was bigger than a Rottweiler and the curly horns atop his handsome head added to his impressive demeanour. As I carefully steered him into the prep room, I feared a caprine catastrophe was imminent. If he escaped, it would be the goat equivalent of a bull in a china shop.

But despite the impression he gave by virtue of his size, penetrating billy goat odour and huge horns, Geoffrey was a model patient. Goats do not respond well to the local anaesthetic that vets use for castrating farm animals, so it is safer to perform the procedure under a full general anaesthetic at the surgery rather than on the farm. We slotted a catheter into the vein in his leg to allow my colleague Helen to keep him asleep. Meanwhile, at the action end, I carefully sliced into the enormous and well-used testicles, removing first one, then the other. Within a few minutes, it was all done. Two testicles, of mango proportions lay on the side as Geoffrey slowly lifted his heavy head and awoke from his slumbers.

Modern anaesthetics can allow a rapid recovery and this is what happened with Geoffrey. He was soon stomping up the ramp of the trailer in which he had arrived, to head back home. But at the practice, a bigger challenge remained, to rid the surgery of the smell of billy goat and mop the floors. It seemed as if he'd sprayed urine into every corner. But worse still, Helen, who had not thought to don her waterproof trousers in advance, found all her clothes were infused with goat urine. She had to resort to wearing surgical scrubs for the rest of the day!

Snowflakes?

We said goodbye to Callum on Friday. Callum is a vet student and a blooming good one, so he is welcome back anytime, to continue to help and to learn, on his way to becoming a fully-fledged veterinary surgeon.

During his fortnight with us, despite having to shove a swab up his nose every morning to ensure he posed no risk of passing on the dreaded lurgy to our staff or clients, Callum was unswervingly enthusiastic about fetching, carrying, cleaning, asking questions and learning. As a third-year student, this was his first placement in practice and he was clearly delighted to be freed from house arrest to do some hands-on practical stuff. He was luckier than most of his cohort of students, many of whom were struggling to find veterinary practices in which to learn.

Our new practice in Thirsk has been busily recruiting new students, too. Another vet student was delighted to have received an affirmative response to her request to come and "see practice" for two weeks.

"Thank you so much," she replied immediately. "So far, you are the first practice to even offer me any dates. I really appreciate it." And the same was true of the student nurse who we met on Thursday. She was desperate to continue her training at college and described the shocking plight of many young people these days: "Half the students on my course will have to abandon it, because there is nowhere for them to get a placement." Needless to say, we are in the process of finding her a spot. And Ed, a young vet who saw practice with me five or six years ago, has just accepted a job at our Wetherby practice. We can't wait to follow his career development as part of our team.

There has been much talk recently of young people forming part of the so-called "snowflake generation". I have to admit I had to look up the meaning of this derogatory term, used by some to describe supposedly delicate and easily offended youngsters. It's pretty offensive and not at all helpful, in my opinion. At a time when the youngest in our society have been locked inside their bedrooms, deprived of proper development and interaction with friends, starved of access to sport and fresh air and proper education, a modern, liberal society should be doing everything it can to assist them. Blaming them for spreading disease (and killing their grannies) surely only serves to alienate them further. It is the responsibility of those of us with age and experience to help them develop into the adults we expect them to be. In the context of the veterinary profession, this means providing students with the opportunities they need to gather the practical experience essential to become competent clinicians and nurses.

I'm writing this on Sunday afternoon having just taken my oldest son to meet a mate so they could go mountain-biking together. It's the first such social meeting for about six months. Of course, they couldn't drive themselves to the car park meeting point, as I would have done when I was the same age, because driving lessons and tests have been cancelled for most of the past twelve months, applying yet more shackles. But neither of them complain. They are both glad of the chance to meet a friend. They set off along the cycle paths at Sutton Bank, enjoying the view and chatting happily, planning their route. There was a stiff north wind, but despite the cold, their laughter seemed to provide a sign that there is hope in the air and in the near future.

So, whatever some people might think or say, the only snowflakes I have seen this week were the ones fluttering from the sky above the Hambleton Hills.

Stifle Solutions

Like football players, dogs are prone to damaging their cruciate ligaments. This short, but strong band of collagen runs inside the stifle joint – the equivalent to the human knee – and keeps it together. This is important because a stifle lacks intrinsic stability. A hip, in contrast, is a ball and socket a bit like a tow bracket for a caravan or trailer. A shoulder has strong extracapsular muscles and tendons that keep everything in place and in the elbow three perfectly sculptured bones interlock precisely to form a perfect hinge. But a stifle comprises the femur (thigh bone) just resting on the tibia (shin bone). The teardrop sliver of the patella, the tiny, mint imperial-like fabellae and the diminutive fibula add to the bony arrangement, but not really to joint stability. Without the integrity of the ligaments inside the joint everything goes wrong.

At vet school, we were taught that, in the fast-moving spaniel who puts his hind foot down a rabbit hole and comes to a sudden stop, forward momentum was the main cause of the injury. The lower part of the limb stays put and the body continues at twenty miles an hour. The poor cruciate ligament doesn't stand a chance. We also see lameness caused by weakness in this area. If the ligament is weak, it can fray or tear even without a sudden with force on the joint. A Rottweiler, sad and toe-touching on his back leg after chasing next door's cat, points an experienced vet immediately to the stifle.

Even before we switch on the X-ray machine, a thorough examination can be enough to make a diagnosis. A fully torn cranial cruciate ligament leaves a slack joint, where the two important

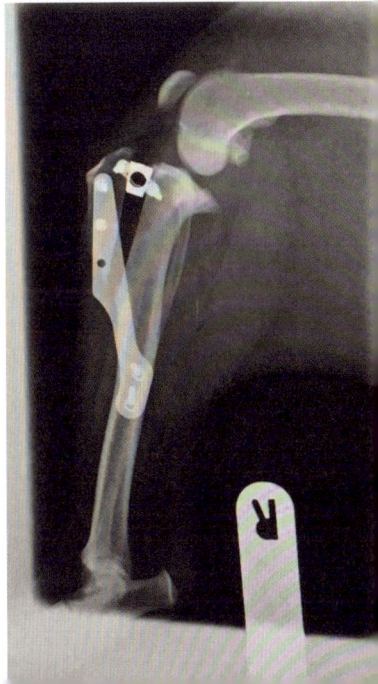

Holly's right leg, after very successful TTA surgery.

bones can be pushed against each other; it's called a *cranial drawer* test. With experience it's easy to appreciate, but it's a technique that is tricky to learn.

The diagnosis might be easy, but the treatment causes bigger problems because there are a multitude of options available. Small dogs with mild injuries can do well with conservative treatment – rest, anti-inflammatories and time – but a complete tear in an energetic, large dog has little chance of resolution without some sort of surgery; at least, not without the development of a degree of osteoarthritis, as the body tries its best to develop some natural stability. It can do so up to a point, but not without long-term pain and disability.

So, for many cruciate ligament injuries, the discussion between the vet and anxious owner turns to the surgical options. There are several alternatives and no one solution stands head and shoulders above the rest. The simplest, called a *lateral suture*, involves adding an artificial nylon ligament, which hugs the stifle and affords an almost immediate stability. It is quite straightforward to perform and relatively inexpensive as the prosthetic ligament is basically a modified version of thick fishing line, its placement and fastening facilitated by some fancy tools. At the other end of the spectrum is the TPLO, or a *tibial plateau levelling osteotomy*, which is as complicated and expensive as it sounds. For various reasons, in part the cost of the kit, it is the technique reserved for specialist orthopaedic surgeons, who can screw together spines and replace hips before lunchtime.

To make decision-making harder still, there is another option, sitting comfortably between basic and top-of-the-range. It's called a TTA and, with fewer letters, it's less expensive than the TPLO. It is fiddly, and requires titanium things but, in my view, for hyperactive springer spaniels, it is most definitely the way forward. For Holly, the energetic springer who had bounced one too many times on her long-suffering cruciate ligament, who I operated on recently, it turned out to be the perfect solution too!

Team Norton Round 2

It was two years ago, almost to the day, when Anne and I operated on Ebony. Then, this elderly alpaca had a growth on her back leg and it demanded a joint effort to sedate her to remove the offending lump. It was challenging, but fortunately everything went to plan. Ebony's cancerous lump was off and it didn't grow back. This week though, it seemed like *déjà vu* as we pondered what to do about another serious-looking marble-sized growth that had appeared to cause Ebony more problems. This new lump was on her face, attached to the lower lip, a whole body away from the previous one.

I hadn't seen the new lump in real life prior to our visit, but I'd scrutinised pictures sent to my phone and I suspected it would need to be removed. For this, as before, I would need another pair of hands. Luckily, for a second time, Anne was available to help. Al fresco procedures like this always bring with them a heady combination of adrenalin and cortisol. They are exciting but, at the same time, there is risk. A second and experienced vet (even if she is your wife) can bring essential confirmation that a challenging operation is the correct course of action. Whilst we might disagree on culinary matters – how long the risotto needs to be cooked for and how much oil or butter or wine needs to be added – we usually agree when it comes to veterinary decisions and that was the case today, with Ebony. My plan, subject to approval, was to sedate Ebony heavily, hoping she would lie down and lie still, instil a local anaesthetic into the nerves to the area, just like at the dentist, then remove the offending tumour and repair the deficit. Once that was done, we needed Ebony to make a steady and controlled recovery from the sedation. It sounded simple but it was a plan fraught with potential pitfalls, all of which we discussed in detail beforehand, hoping we had everything covered.

I calculated the dose of sedative and, fortunately, hit the vein first time. Ebony obligingly followed the textbook, although there isn't really a textbook for alpacas, and she drifted off into a deep sleep. Next was the nerve block – an injection via a long thin needle, with the technical description of being "medial to the mandibular ramus" to block the crucial mandibular nerve. This was followed by another nerve block at a different site – the unusually named "mental foramen". This was technically termed, at least by me, as a "mental block". It caused amusement for several minutes.

But back to the patient: Ebony was fast asleep and her lip was comfortably numbed. Anne, keeping an eye on the alpaca's sedation, clipped and scrubbed the site while I prepared my surgical kit before finally taking a deep breath and making the first cut. It was a deep one, followed by another deep one and within a minute or so the offending lump was off. Ebony, just as she had two years ago, lay still and fast asleep, oblivious to the surgical action on her face. As I reached for my sutures, Anne's reassuring nod that our patient was doing well was needed. I repaired the gaping cleft

in Ebony's lip as deftly as the early morning chilly temperature in the barn would allow; another challenge of outdoor surgery. Before long, Ebony's lip looked as good as new. I swabbed the blood clots from her woolly chin and we rocked back on our heels, extending our backs and anxiously awaiting her recovery.

But we needn't have worried. For a second time, Ebony bounced back with vigour.

Monty Don

Recently I have been reeling from the olfactory effects of my dog's new habit of rolling in smelly substances, particularly hedgehog poo. However, this habit is nowhere near as offensive as that of Monty, the fluffy chocolate cocker spaniel, who was just three months old when he came rushing in for his second vaccination. A more perfect picture of canine cuteness could not have been imagined and, as I fussed over him from the opposite side my perennial COVID-deterring mask, Monty licked my face with vigour.

"We call him Monty after Monty Don, because he loves being out in the garden," explained Monty's owner, as I reached for the vials of vaccine.

Second vaccination appointments are the best. The main clinical examination has already been done, so it is a chance to talk about the development of a young dog whose life, health and accidents I might be following for the next decade. But today, the answers to the usual questions about the pup's progress revealed something rather nasty.

"He's doing well, growing up nicely and getting bigger and stronger, but he has a terrible habit of eating his own poo. I don't know how to stop it!" reported his affectionate, but conflicted, owner. The technical name for this behaviour is coprophagia. It is as serious as its name suggests and often hard to fix. Solving the problem revolves around breaking the bad habit. Some advice suggests adding garlic/chillies/pineapple juice to the diet in order to make the faeces taste horrible. It stretches comprehension to imply that the faeces do not taste horrible enough already, and that the addition of strong flavours might deter a dog from this disgusting habit. I've never found it works and tactics like using a muzzle for short periods pre- and post-defaecation and fastidiously removing extruded excrement before there is any chance for a faecal feast are often most effective.

Monty's mum described the challenge she was facing.

"Monty makes it hard for us, because he rushes into the garden and heads into one corner. He passes some poo, then I go and collect it in a bag. But while I'm picking it up, he rushes to another corner, passes more poo and then eats it before I have chance to get to him. I don't know what to do!"

It was a desperate plea for help in the sorry tale of Monty and his horrible habit. I could picture the scene and it brought back the ugly memory of a client who described a pup who would not only eat its own faeces, but would also follow its canine friend around on a walk, waiting for an extra snack, which was even more gross.

We talked though the problem and possible ways to deal with it, and I sympathised, concurring that my own dog had developed her own smelly habits. I urged a determined approach – maybe a circuit breaker lockdown of this antisocial behaviour might work? This is one occasion where it is a shame that a simple conversation isn't one of the options. "Monty, this seems strange to me," might be the approach. "If you see faeces when you're out or in the garden, just walk on by," was surely great advice.

I drew up the vaccine, which I needed to inject to keep Monty safe from infectious diseases, fussed his fluffy head and tried not to think about what had probably passed his lips earlier that morning. Monty continued wagging his tail, totally unaware of the needle. As if to thank me for being gentle, he turned around and vigorously licked my face. For once, I felt very happy to be wearing a face covering!

Meeting Rossdale

I had a serendipitous encounter before recent lockdowns. An old friend called John came to see me at the end of morning surgery. There was nothing new about this because I had known John for years and he would always appear, with a Norfolk terrier bundled under his arm like a rugby ball, way after surgery should have finished. This always made me late because I liked talking to John and listening to his stories of the halcyon days of veterinary practice – his father had been a horse vet in Newmarket once upon a time. I could happily pass an hour during a busy day listening to anecdotes about Twink Allen and other famous vets who John and his father knew.

Today, though, John had no terrier under his arm. Instead he held a slip of paper with his phone number on.

"A mate of mine is visiting Yorkshire and he wants to go for lunch with you and your wife," he said as he thrust the piece of paper into my hand. "He's a massive fan and loves your books," he added. "It's Peter Rossdale. Give me a ring if you can come."

If you were to make a list of the most significant vets of the last century, Peter Rossdale would be in the top five. He set up the most iconic and famous veterinary practice of them all: Rossdale's in Newmarket. As an enthusiastic student at Cambridge, just down the road from Newmarket, I was very well acquainted with this place, but only the very finest equine students would be accepted to spend a few weeks learning there and only the crème de la crème needed to consider applying for an internship.

During the early episodes of *The Yorkshire Vet*, when we were suddenly exposed to an unexpected level of public comment, criticism along the lines of "You shouldn't do it like that!" or "Why didn't you do a blood test on that poorly cat?" or "A first-opinion vet in general practice shouldn't be attempting that kind of surgery – it's a job for the specialists" were, while uncommon, frequent enough to cause me anxiety. But I also received the occasional letter from Dr Rossdale and, when it felt that there was overwhelming public scrutiny on my practice and my practise, to receive positive comments from a veterinary titan was both humbling and reassuring.

Needless to say, when invited to a lunchtime meeting with Peter Rossdale, I put everything on hold and, with great excitement, headed to the excellent Stapylton Arms in Wass. My old friend John and my new friend Peter, their respective wives and I enjoyed a superb meal and chatted about all things veterinary, both current and historic. As coffee was ordered and our lovely meal drew to a close, I put to Peter the question I had been burning to ask. Out of all his amazing achievements during his illustrious veterinary career, what did he consider his most significant achievement? I expected his reply would be the discovery of a new diagnostic test for a sick neonatal foal or a novel treatment for equine endometritis or something similar and specific. He paused for a moment before giving an understated response.

"Well, I suppose I was the first vet who espoused and practised the concept of 'evidence-based medicine'."

Current veterinary journals and modern "experts" use this phrase with abandon. It is the mantra of twenty-first-century veterinary practice. But Peter Rossdale had conceived and instigated that way of working many years ahead of its time. I was privileged to have enjoyed a lovely lunch with a great man. It was affirming on many levels.

Extending Leads and Retractable Puppies

When I set about writing my weekly column, whether it's late at night and at the last minute, or organised and well in advance, I always give it a title. It keeps me focused on what I've decided to write about. Of course, the title doesn't appear in the newspaper – it simply says: "Julian Norton *The Yorkshire Vet*". This is a shame, because I sometimes think the title is the best bit. Among my favourite titles are *Châteauneuf-du-Hamster* (which featured a hamster restrained in a wine glass, so I could examine it without getting bitten) and *Reel around the Fountain (*which is the title of a classic Smith's song, but also described my encounter with a nervous dog by the fountain in the centre of Boroughbridge).

Today's piece is entitled, at least in the file on my laptop, *Extending Leads and Retractable Puppies* and describes something I experienced this morning, whilst walking my own dog, Emmy. We'd just completed our usual circumnavigation of Sowerby Flatts. This lovely area of open space provides grazing for a few dozen tame bullocks and a dog-walking haven for the people of Thirsk and Sowerby. There is an endless combination of loops on either side of the gently meandering Cod Beck, which has kingfishers and herons but definitely no cod. One part of this little river is very straight after a half-hearted attempt to turn it into a canal. Over the years that I have lived in Sowerby, I've

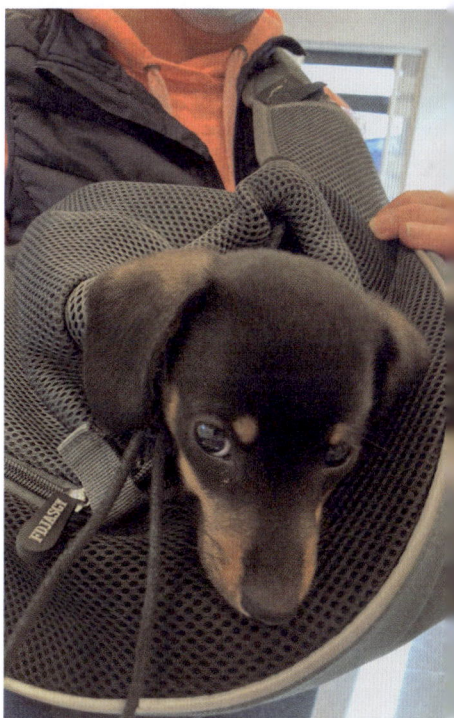

Another baby, miniature dachshund, this one in a bag, not on an extendable-retractable lead

observed the beck's gentle but persistent determination to return to its original course. One day, I hope it will make it back. On a warm day, the grazing cattle often stand cooling their feet in a shallow part. On a hot day, children paddle and even swim. But, before work, it is the domain of the dog walker. This morning, one little chap was out, I guessed, for his first ever walk. He was so small that he must have only just had the necessary vaccinations. He was a miniature dachshund and he gamely entered the fields via the kissing gate, eventually followed by his owner, who was connected to him via a huge retractable and extendable lead. The mini dog was full of excitement and his long, curled tail pointed upwards and twirled round madly. If it went much faster, I reckoned he'd take off like a helicopter. Emmy and I watched from a distance as he ran in all directions, unaware of the presence of a proper path to follow. It was a comical sight, because the dog was so small and the extendable lead was so long, but the owner was happy in the knowledge that his new puppy would be safe and could not run off or get lost. But the way the new owner stared at the controlling handle of the lead made me think he was a novice at using such a complicated device.

I remember when these extendable–retractable leads were first invented. My gran, who had bred dogs all her life and ran a small boarding kennels and therefore knew everything about dogs, disapproved of the new-fangled things. It was impossible to control the dog properly at its far end. To her, a short length of rope was perfect. This morning, the limitations identified decades earlier by my gran were evident. When a big, fluffy dog approached the tiny pooch, the new owner either panicked or deliberately pressed the "retract" button to bring his puppy back to safety. Sadly, the combination of the small mass of the baby dachshund and the power of the elastic recoil in the lead succeeded in sending the puppy hurtling through midair. He landed, confused but fortunately not injured, at his dad's feet moments later. For once, the extendable–retractable lead had exercised far too much control!

An Old Tortoise

This week I examined the oldest patient ever to have entered my consulting room. He was a tortoise and that was also his name, "Tortoise". Wendy, his initially reluctant owner, had inherited him many years before, when a neighbour had died. She was the next chelonian custodian. Tortoise's future was also guaranteed, because he was written into Wendy's will, covering the eventuality that he might also outlive his second owner.

He had recently emerged from hibernation – the bangs and scratching from the box in the attic had alerted Wendy to his awakening. But the alternating cold and warm weather had confused the cold-blooded creature. Instead of warming under the sun's rays on a warm May morning, Tortoise was sluggish and his appetite poor, which was why he'd come to see me. I lifted him from the wicker, punnet-style basket in which he'd arrived. Under his picnic blanket, he looked like a crusty pie prepared for a summer picnic. He was big and heavy. I started to ask the questions that would help me decide upon a course of action.

It turned out he was almost certainly over one hundred years old. It also turned out he was a character. Over the decades, he had regularly escaped, only to re-appear in all corners of the village where he lived. He was a local celebrity, known to everyone of all generations.

I once knew a tortoise which was so fast and adept at escaping and then hiding, that his owner glued, using araldite, a long flagpole to the top of his shell. That way he was easily identifiable even in the depths of the herbaceous border. I suggested the idea to Wendy, who didn't look convinced.

I conducted my examination feeling a great weight of responsibility. This happens to vets when they examine a child's favourite pet, a farmer's prize tup or bull or an elderly pony which has taught a long line of youngsters to ride. Of course, we have a natural urgency to cure *all* patients, but in some cases, there feels an extra pressure from the responsibility of caring for such an elderly animal.

The first thing I always do with a tortoise, once I've lifted him from the table and eyed him up and down, is measure the carapace, or shell, with a ruler. Then I put him on the scales and calculate something called the *Jackson ration*. This gives a good indication whether the weight is good, or too low. In other animals, vets can lay their hands on and try to feel ribs or bones of the back to assess the body condition. Hidden under an impenetrable shell, this is never possible in a tortoise. Luckily, the ruler/weighing scales combination gives a good indication of general condition.

The rest of the examination is more difficult, focusing mainly on the bits that stick out from under the shell – the head and legs. Today, the eyes were bright, the limbs moved vigorously and freely and the mouth was healthy and free from infection or disease. I reached for my standard tortoise multivitamin injection and hoped it would do its thing. If this didn't work, the next stage for an anorexic tortoise is intensive care, involving regular bathing in warm water, stomach-tubing with special recovery diet, blood tests and even X-rays. I suspected Tortoise had seen this all before and would bounce back once the proper weather returned.

"And do you think he'll be mended by June?" asked Wendy. "It's just that we are going on holiday to Cornwall then and Tortoise is coming with us. It's a long journey on the train and he'll have to come too." It was evident that the centenarian had plenty more adventures left.

Dogs Who Look Like People

It is inexplicably true that many dogs look like their owners. Or maybe it's the owners who look like their dogs. Nobody knows why this is the case, but there are numerous examples. The wiry fell runner with a rough, lanky lurcher; a stocky bodybuilder with his equally squat-of-stature bulldog; or the scruffy farmer, trousers fastened by bailer twine, accompanied by an unkempt collie with exactly the same basic but functional farm string in use as a makeshift lead. All have found, probably unwittingly, a kindred spirit in appearance as well as attitude.

One day this week, Bodhi the poodle cross came in to see me. Suffering from a bad bout of diarrhoea, he was subdued and lethargic and, at this time, did not embody the Sanskrit origins and spirit of his name: enlightened and empowered.

After the usual greetings with the new client, I couldn't help but quiz Bodhi's owner about his name.

"Is that Bodhi as in '*if you want the ultimate, you've gotta be willing to pay the ultimate price*'," I wondered, "because he does look *exactly* like him."

The Bodhi I was referring to was the surfing bank robber-cum-adrenaline junky played by the late Patrick Swayze in the absolute classic cult nineties film *Point Break*.

Bodhi the poodle, with his fuzzy, curling and flowing locks really did look exactly like the eponymous star, but I suspected the film might not be well known amongst the dog-owning demographic of Wetherby and braced myself for

Bodhi, waiting patiently for the Fifty-Year Storm. *Or maybe just his diarrhoea-solving injection.*

an awkward and unknowing silence. I decided that a transient embarrassment was worth the risk when weighed up against the possibility of finding a fellow fan. So, I was pleasantly surprised by an answer in the affirmative.

"Yes, he is!" exclaimed his owner. "*Point Break* is my favourite film and I've always wanted a dog that looked like Patrick Swayze!" I was delighted that I hadn't made another fool of myself and I looked down to the bouffant dog to make another mental comparison. Despite the diarrhoea, his appealing eyes looked happy and his tail wagged constantly, so I knew he wasn't too poorly. I had ample opportunity to postpone the clinical chat and examination and talk to a fellow enthusiast about the film. We compared best lines and bemoaned the lack of universal popularity of such a great piece of cinema. Eventually, I had to lift Bodhi onto the table to examine him.

"You still surfing?" I imagined him asking. In my mind, I replied, "Every day."

I quickly snapped out of my Bell's Beach daydream and got on with the task in hand. Bodhi had a simple case of gastroenteritis, which was the reason for his week-long illness and nocturnal kitchen explosions. It would be straightforward to make him feel better and I administered the appropriate drugs. I snapped Bodhi's photo – it was the closest I'd get to meeting a film star and it would make a light-hearted Instagram post, even if not many people knew what I was on about when I mentioned the "Fifty-year storm". Bodhi's owner promised to send me some additional photos – apparently, there were loads where he looked even more like the swashbuckling hero. Sure enough, later that day, my phone pinged with a veritable album of Bodhi photographs. In some, the setting sun reflected off his curly locks as he gazed into the distance. At the end of the photo album, there was a sentence which made my job worthwhile.

"Many thanks for looking after Bodhi. He is a lot better already x"

Maremma and Hens

I met an interesting patient a few months ago. The relaxed and laconic dog looked, to the untrained eye, like a long-haired and pale golden retriever. But I was quickly enlightened by her devoted owner – she was, in fact, an unusual and amazing breed called a Maremma-Abruzzese sheepdog. The fascinating thing about these dogs, which hail from Italy, is that their role in helping sheep does not involve rounding them up from hills into smaller paddocks or pens like the classic sheepdogs in this country. Rather, they protect the flock from attack by wolves or other predators, by mixing amongst the sheep. From a distance they must look just like part of the woolly flock. There are other breeds that do the same thing: the Anatolian, which once had a similar role in Turkey, is now achieving great success warding off (and therefore protecting) cheetahs from flocks and herds and farmers in Namibia. The Pyrenean mountain dog and the Polish tatra sheepdog historically do the same job. These livestock guardian dogs have an amazing heritage but, like many traditional roles, have become largely redundant over recent years, as predators such as wild wolves and bears have disappeared.

As I discussed the fascinating history of the Maremmas in my consulting room, it transpired that the role of livestock guarding dogs has been revived much closer to home than the Anatolians in Namibia. Just outside Halifax, there is a free-range chicken farm where hens roam the grassy slopes of the Pennines, enjoying fresh air and a wholesome life, whilst laying eggs in abundance. Having been blighted by fox attacks, which had decimated the flock, Danni and her husband had looked for a sustainable and humane solution. They found Bear and Lina, a pair of Maremmas. Lina was a rescued dog and Bear arrived as a puppy. The two immediately formed a bond and Bear learnt from the older dog, who knew just what she needed to do. My interest was piqued and I decided that, if I could find some spare time, I would go and visit this farm, to see the dogs in action.

And so, a couple of weeks ago, I headed through Halifax to see Danni, Bear and Lina and Danni's flock of hens, to learn about Maremmas and witness their guarding first-hand. On a sunny day, cotton wool clouds shared a sapphire sky and the sloped grassy paddocks, peppered with hens, looked like a scene from the Alps. Danni pointed out the fluffy guarding dogs in the distance, as they sat surveying the scene. With noses in the air, they quickly sensed someone had arrived near the hens and came to investigate.

"I'll put Lina away," said Danni, explaining. "She's very protective of the flock and doesn't like strangers."

But Bear was more relaxed and came to say hello. Danni told me about the problem they had experienced with foxes. I could see why. The perimeter boundary consisted of a drystone wall. Even with extra reinforcements and electric fencing, a wily fox would find a way into the hen field. And that's where the Maremmas came in. I could see a well-worn track around the outside of the field. Danni explained that the dogs walked round the edge of the field each morning and evening, checking its integrity. Then, they'd position themselves on a high vantage point so that they could survey the whole field for intruders.

"One year we lost 700 birds. Since we've had the dogs, we haven't lost any!" confirmed Danni, with delight. It was a truly holistic approach to farm security and animal safety.

Bear supervising his flock (of hens).

Sheep's Eye

I've been out and about over the last couple of weeks, helping other vets by offering another pair of hands, as well as advice from experience. My first excursion was to the depths of West Yorkshire. As I made my way off the M62, winding up and down lanes, which got narrower and narrower, the traffic got less and the scenery became greener. It brought back plenty of memories from my youth, when I knew many of these lanes like the back of my hand. I'm still fascinated by the amalgamation of peaceful rural scenes alongside railways, roads and canals in this area. There is a rich history of agriculture and industry in West Yorkshire.

Matt the vet had asked for some help with an alpaca, who was suffering from a dramatic scaly and scabby skin condition around its mouth. He'd done lots of investigative tests – biopsies and blood tests – and started some treatment. Whilst the treatment had improved the problem, Matt wanted another set of eyes and another opinion on a species he was not so familiar with. I love alpacas and so I was happy to assist.

With the air of an expert (which I am not), I surveyed the patient from a sensible distance and asked the owner questions to get an idea of the problem. Matt's tests had helped, but it was clear that we'd have to get up close to examine the skin around the mouth and also have a look inside. I donned the customary latex gloves and started my hands-on inspection. Before long, we'd identified part

of the problem, which was simple to resolve. If you're a fan of *The Yorkshire Vet* I'll not spoil the surprise and the answer to the problem prematurely…

My second secondment was to help a former colleague and friend, who was also looking for guidance. Katy had a problem with a sheep. Or rather, the sheep had a problem with its eye. First it was phone advice, followed by the scrutinising of photos sent by WhatsApp. The horribly damaged eye had stubbornly refused to respond to the normal treatments. "Does it need to be removed?" was the all-important question she posed. I agreed: it seemed that enucleation (removal of the eyeball) was the only option to relieve the painful swelling and soreness. The next question: could I come along and help?

I've worked with Katy for more years than either of us can remember. She's brilliant, compassionate and full of enthusiasm. I still think of her as a young member of our profession, but she has skills beyond her years and is accomplished in all aspects of mixed practice. I was flattered to be asked to help her when she performed her first ever ovine orbital operation.

It's a challenging procedure and not one for the faint-hearted. There is a lot that can go wrong and good preparation, slick surgical technique and a calm manner are all important. Luckily, we had (at least some of) these properties in abundance. It turned out that the hardest part of the evening's job, completed after both our normal working days had finished, was capturing the patient. Her lamb skipped and gambolled, oblivious to his mum's plight as she ran around the fold yard. Eventually, under sedation and after the copious infusion of local anaesthetic, Katy readied her equipment and steadied her nerves. My role was to offer help and advice along the way, but just before Katy made her first cut I decided I should come clean. In twenty-five years of practising, I'd never removed an eyeball from a sheep, so she was as experienced as I was.

River Adventure

Last weekend's action had been months in the making. Our enthusiastic and like-minded friend Lucy had hatched a plan for a river adventure. It was a toned-down version of plan A which we had all dreamt up at the end of a drunken dinner party and, as such, would never have worked. That one involved an expeditionary force of two stand-up-paddleboards leaving Thirsk, navigating Cod Beck, meeting the Swale and eventually arriving at Spurn Point at the mouth of the Humber. It would surely have been an epic adventure but, in the sober light of day, we realised it was not quite the great idea we had first thought. Detailed analysis of my stand-up-paddleboard speed and (lack of) skills during a previous aquatic escapade on the River Tees revealed that this adventure would take several days. The watered-down and much more realistic version that we settled upon involved a fleet of kayaks and SUPs paddling from the lovely little village of Beningbrough, through York to Naburn beyond. It was a 20-kilometre trek, all downstream. As we inflated our craft and assembled the flotilla, we all felt as if we were part of a *Swallows and Amazons* story.

We set off shortly after noon, with emergency bananas, water and suncream. Once we'd got used to our craft, it quickly became clear that progress would be slow. Although, at the start of the journey there were no riverside paths or people, it was evident we were travelling at approximately walking pace. However, unlike a walk along the river, there was the added excitement inherent in the ever present risk of falling in. The kayakers, Anne and Archie included, seemed to fair best. The paddleboarders – Jack and I – coped, but one of us (by which I mean me) struggled with unpredictable wash from the occasional motorised boats. Several times I found myself wobbling precariously and dropping to my knees for security. It was pointed out that my board had a noticable sag in the centre. Either I hadn't pumped it up enough, or I was too heavy for the board. At one terrible moment, right in the centre of York, as we passed the

Museum Gardens and in front of all the al fresco drinkers relaxing at the riverside bars, I capsized. Luckily, it was near the bank and shallow enough for me to stand up and easily remount my board.

There was another minor crisis when one of the double kayaks appeared to be losing air. The sides seemed floppy, its pace dropped and it started to take on water. An emergency stop to bail out and some vigorous pumping solved the problem, at least for a while.

Despite hiccups, our flotilla made steady progress, but it was hot and we were starting to flag – not because of the pace but because we'd been paddling for hours. Then, like a mirage in the desert, we spotted something in the distance. "Is that a floating icecream van, moored on the bank of the river?" we asked ourselves. Surely we were hallucinating, dehydrated and short of energy (bananas having been consumed two hours earlier, at the time of the crisis of the deflating kayak).

But it was real. An icecream-van-boat was moored on the far bank and we paddled furiously across the stream, brandishing the stashed – and luckily now waterproof – ten pound notes, secreted for emergencies. The icecream-van-boat had two windows. The starboard window faced the park, where a long queue of land-lubbers waited in line for their 99s. We sidled up to the window to port that opened onto the river, egregiously jumping the queue. Tubs of icecream and lollies boosted our energy reserves and saved the day. It had truly been an excellent adventure. Next time a trip to Spurn Point?

Boos on the Beach

I had an appointment at a literary festival last weekend. I was excited. The event was part of the "Books on the Beach" festival held in Scarborough. It is a really fantastic festival, superbly organised and always very popular. I was last there a couple of years ago and I had a great time, so it was good to be able to support the event again.

But the most exciting part was that it marked the first "in person" event I had attended for over a year. At last, I would be able to talk to an actual audience, rather than the pixelated and remote faces in boxes on a Zoom screen, to which we have all become accustomed. Instead, there would be the human interaction everyone needs to thrive. Where there is a live audience there is an atmosphere. Even though these events are not a natural environment for me, I couldn't wait.

Last year's festival had been cancelled, for obvious reasons. It was rearranged for the spring, but this too had to be postponed. There were multiple crossings out and scribbles in my diary and I had almost forgotten about the whole thing. But, two weeks ago, an email arrived from my publisher reminding me that, at last, it was going ahead. The email gave me more details of the event, timings and postcodes. The uncharacteristic typo in the first line of the email did not fill me with confidence. It said, "Boos on the Beach". I hoped it *was* a typo and that the audience would not be subjecting me to disgruntled heckling during my first book festival for a while.

After so long with nothing happening at the weekends, it turned out I had a clash of engagements. Our kids were rowing in Durham Regatta. Again, it was one of the first sporting events for over a year and I didn't want to miss that either. Luckily, the racing was held over two days, so my departure shortly after lunchtime on Sunday meant I only missed three out of the eighteen races in which Jack and Archie were involved.

The next job was working out a sensible route from Durham to Scarborough. This was no mean feat, even with the aid of the Internet. In my head, it was reasonably close. In reality, it was nothing of the sort. Having circumnavigated industrial Teesside and traversed the moors, the sea eventually appeared. It took almost two hours. By the time I arrived, Anne had sent me multiple updates of the results of heats, semi-finals and finals, so I was abreast of the progress in Durham. What I didn't know at this point was the size of the audience in Scarborough. Would it be worth the journey and missing the racing fun, or would there be five people and a dog? On a sunny Sunday, wouldn't people be actually on the beach, with their books, buckets or spades? Would the rules of the people/distance equation mean that the auditorium could only be one third full?

But I need not have worried. The audience was as replete as rules would allow and I chatted beforehand, even signing some autographs. Gerry, my interlocutor for the afternoon, asked probing questions and provided a perfect springboard for anecdotes and amusing stories. The hour flew by and before long it was time for questions from the floor before signings of my recent book *All Creatures: Heart-warming Tales from a Yorkshire Vet* (available from all good bookshops!). It was good to be back and, thankfully, without a single boo! There was good news from the tail-end of the regatta, too, with two firsts and four seconds from the younger Nortons. It had been a good weekend.

A Pair of Socks

Saturday mornings are one of my favourite times of the week. A weekend without work can take on many shapes: a relaxing and protracted breakfast, plenty of coffee and *The Yorkshire Post Country Week* is one pleasant way to recover from the previous five days. Equally, a mountain biking adventure with the boys is hard to beat. But when on duty, working a Saturday can be better than the other five days put together. There are fewer staff so, if it's quiet, a sort of party atmosphere can develop. If busy (and nobody can predict these things) then the smaller team is drawn into unified action, working closely together, like a well-oiled machine.

My last Saturday was already fully booked with appointments by halfway through Friday, so Lucy, Sarah and I expected we would be busy. With very little space to slot in the possible morning emergencies, we would all have to be on top form. Just after ten minutes, one such emergency cropped up. A Labrador puppy had swallowed a sock. "I know he ate it because I saw him pick it up," explained his distraught owner. "And then he swallowed it before I could grab it."

The puppy was rushed down to fit in as an extra. He looked very healthy and extremely pleased with himself, having outwitted (or so he thought) a human and eaten some of her footwear. The other, uneaten sock was brought along for me to gauge the size and likely implications. I weighed up the options:

i)   Leave sock to see if it would pass through – a risky strategy. I'd seen some socks do this, emerging in a smellier state than they had entered, but there were plenty that got lodged in the stomach or intestines, leading to a crisis.

ii) Give drugs to induce vomiting – a sensible strategy, until the vomiting pup fails to produce a sock, in which case the fraught vet has to operate on a dog who has just vomited eight times. I've regretted this course of action on several occasions.

iii)   Attempt to remove the sock by endoscope – good in theory, but may take more than an hour, if the grabbers don't grab. It can be impossible if the sock has already moved out of the stomach.

iv)   Operate to surgically remove the offending sock directly from the stomach – this requires surgery but will resolve the problem in a predictable and foolproof way.

Needless to say, after some thought and discussion, I opted for the last one.

Before long, a fetid sock, stained with gastric juices, swollen and much bigger than the other part of its pair, was sitting in a kidney dish as the little dog raised his head in recovery, slightly confused about what had just happened.

The dream-team continued its work and just before home time, Sarah put another phone call on hold. "You're not going to believe this. I have the owner of another puppy on the phone. She's just swallowed a sock. What shall I tell her?"

"You'd better ask her to bring her down," I said, and we readied theatre. It felt like Groundhog Day.

The second surgery was almost identical and went smoothly too. Whilst stitching up, we reminisced about interesting foreign body removals we'd seen. One story went like this:

"We'd removed some lady's underwear from a dog's intestines. The owners came in to collect the patient and I handed the dog over as well the pants in a plastic bag. The wife suddenly shouted, 'They are not *my* pants!' The husband went very quiet and they left in a hurry!"

Evidently, that one didn't have such a happy outcome…

Ratatouille

We've had an invasion of rats in the practice recently. Not the ones which would lead you to search for help from pest control, but the friendly pet versions. They are brilliant pets and their innate curiosity and obvious affection for humans is captivating. Rat owners, too, are great because they have an enthusiasm for these rodents which is almost unrivalled amongst the animal-owning community. The combination of interesting patients and passionate owners is hard to beat.

One day recently, we had eighteen of them, all being weighed and checked for health prior to two big events. One was the introduction of six new baby rats; the other was the arrival of a brand-new rodent house, complete with places for burrowing tunnels. Both would be exciting but just as when we humans move house, potentially stressful. I was introduced to the rats one by one. I was slightly disappointed not to find any were called "Roland", after the famous 1980s TV rat. Instead, they all had names from science fiction films. Two had lumps, which I deemed sufficiently suspicious to advise they should be removed. It's not a very easy thing to do, partly because of the small size of the rat and partly because anaesthesia is not so simple. Emma the owner was anxious but pragmatic about the risk. She was also practical to the point of having already organised some collars to stop them licking their wounds. These plastic devices are often used on

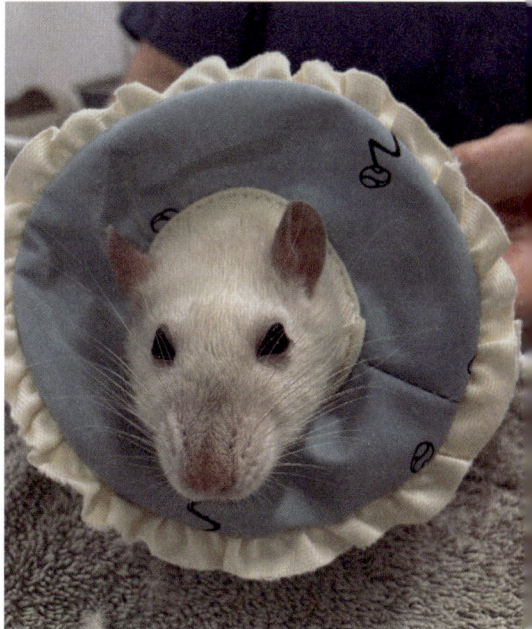

dogs or cats to stop them interfering with op sites, intravenous drips or catheters. I've talked about them previously in this column and they are a whole topic in themselves. The ones Emma presented were made of cloth, floppy and in pastel shades. You could imagine the "mice on the mouse organ" in *Bagpuss* wearing them. One was pale yellow and I joked that the rat who wore it would look like a primrose. But that was for later. First, I needed to get on with the surgery. Before Emma departed, she handed over various snacks and nibbles for the rats after their surgery (rat snacks). One was a tube of tasty paste. She gave very specific instructions: "When you give them this you must say 'lick'. It's very important." I nodded and made a mental note, although I couldn't imagine a little rat would have sufficient vocabulary or ability to follow instructions to make this relevant. I headed towards theatre, hoping all would go to plan.

Before long rat number one, whose name was Dax, was recovering on the table and the lump was off. We tried all the floppy collars, one at a time. Each of them made the rat look like a flower, but none of them stayed in place for more than a few seconds. Abandoning that idea, I searched for the rat snacks and Dax tucked in hungrily. Finally, I smeared a blob of the rat paste on my finger and held it out for tasting. I'd forgotten the very specific instructions I'd been given and didn't say the magic word "lick". The next thing that happened was very sharp and very painful and similar to Richard Whiteley's experience on *Calendar* many years ago. That was a ferret and it wasn't his finger, but as the Taser-like pain continued to course up the nerves from my finger to my spine, I could empathise. Calm was eventually restored, with a combination of swabs, plasters and tissue glue and I tried to clean my own blood off the rat. Was it my failure to follow the simple instructions of asking him to "lick" or had I caused unnecessary offence by dressing him as a flower? I'll never know.

Bouffant

The waiting room was already at capacity and because of this – and also because the patient had a cough, suspicious of a canine respiratory disease almost as infectious as pesky COVID – I headed out to find Alfie in the car park. We've seen a few cases of infectious tracheitis recently and it's better to not have a coughing dog in the waiting room, where infection can pass to other dogs. Similar to whooping cough in children, infectious tracheitis can be a nuisance. It causes a dramatic and harsh cough, just as if something is stuck in the throat, and often culminates in a wretch of frothy mucous. Dogs rarely seem to feel very poorly with this disease, which is caused by a mix of viruses along with a bacterium called *Bordatella*, although puppies and older dogs can be more seriously affected. It is simple to diagnose and easy to treat, although the irritation can persist for some time.

We'd seen this little dog regularly at the practice over recent months, because of a persistently sore eye. He was well known and well liked. The little Bichon Frise was very cute but he stubbornly resisted all attempts to treat his eye. The delightful ball of cotton wool turned into a whirling dervish when approached with eye-drops, so it was all hands on deck.

Fortunately, the eye condition was resolved several months ago and a happy relationship with the vet had been resumed. But today he was coughing and I searched the car park for a small, white fluffy dog looking out of the car window. Not one was to be seen. In one vehicle a barking hound that looked like a standard poodle, frothed at the inside of the window as I approached. I turned and went to look elsewhere, to no avail. I couldn't find Alfie anywhere. Maybe he'd gone for a walk? Maybe a colleague was seeing him? I called my next client in.

But Alfie was still highlighted on the screen as *waiting to be seen*, so I returned to the car park a second time. This time, Alfie's owner was standing outside the car, trying to attract my attention.

"Sorry, I didn't see you there," I apologised. "I saw a dog but it looked much bigger than little Alfie – I thought he was a large poodle."

His owner was opening the back door for Alfie to leap out.

"Well, he's just been to the groomers for a bath and trim and shampoo, so his ears and head are very fluffy," he explained. "And the other thing is, he always gets static from travelling in the car, so his hair stands on end. He looks much bigger than usual when he's inside the car!"

Sure enough, little Alfie stood there, fluffed up like a frightened cat, twice his normal size but oblivious to his exaggerated proportions. I bent down to stroke him prior to my examination with a stethoscope but, at the last moment, changed my mind.

"Will I get an electric shock if I touch him?" I asked, just to check. But, of course, I didn't. As he walked around on the ground, the electric charge obviously dissipated because his bouffant hairdo subsided to the level of a normal dog after a grooming. I listened to his chest and windpipe where, sure enough, there was a rasping noise on a par with Darth Vader's breathing. Gentle manipulation of the larynx confirmed a super-sensitivity and he coughed on cue; it was simple to make a diagnosis.

As I went inside with Alfie's owner to organise the medication he'd need, we chatted and laughed about the amusing hair. "What happens when the weather gets humid? I bet he's even bigger then?"

Pot on a Lamb and Goitre in a Boar

Last Tuesday was a bit like the old days, when being a vet in Yorkshire genuinely involved all creatures of all sizes. Times have certainly changed for me, as they have for many veterinary surgeons and veterinary practices. Twenty-five years ago, just about all veterinarians offered a very mixed range of services, because market towns were surrounded by agricultural land where farmers and their animals flourished in abundance. Now, whether we like it or not, there are many fewer farms, but there are also many more dogs and cats, which demand a more complex level of care than once was the case. Times have, subtly, changed.

My morning had been busy with small animals at our practice in Wetherby. Consulting sounds straightforward. In some ways, it is. There are no moments of high stress when a crucial incision or saw cut is required, or if a ligature slips off a pulsating artery. But consulting is intense in a different way. A full list of consultations requires complete concentration with many decisions to be made and clear communication required at every stage.

Henry was my final case. He was suffering from an inoperable rectal tumour that I was treating with metronomic chemotherapy – this sounds fancy but really it isn't. It is a way to control a cancer using tablets rather than surgery or brightly coloured intravenous infusions. Henry's wagging tail told me much of what I needed

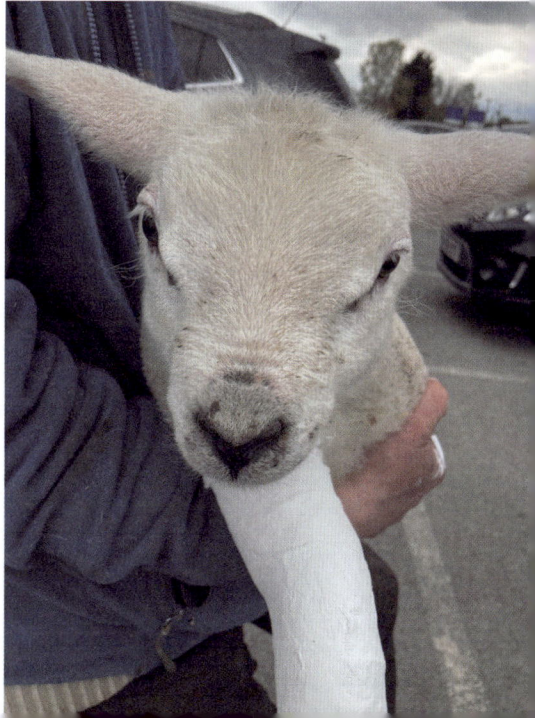

to know before I set about assessing his lump or taking his blood. He was responding very well.

Having dealt with my small animal patients, I headed out towards the open spaces of the moors. I had a pig to see. It was a huge boar with a melon-sized mass in its lower neck. I'd seen photos but today was the first time I would clap eyes on the lump. I'd met the boar, whose name was Hal, some years before. He had been brought over from the Netherlands to introduce some much-needed extra genes into the rare-breed herd, and I was on the farm when he arrived. Age had crept up on Hal and the lump sounded serious. My job was to try and find out what it was and work out what to do. A lump on a farm animal, as any fan of *The Yorkshire Vet* will know, is likely to be an abscess. So, plan A was to perform a Fine Needle Aspirate. Today's attempt, in an uncooperative Mangalitza pig, was not exactly fine, but it achieved what was needed. The total absence of pus, but an abundance of blood ruled out an abscess but hinted towards a vascular mass. Given its position, I suspected a thyroid growth. Could this be an enlarged thyroid gland? Did Hal have a goitre? Could he have low iodine levels? It was certainly possible and I set about extracting a blood sample to check.

Back at the Thirsk practice, Lindsay our head nurse looked at my sample with some consternation. "This is from a pig. Can you find a lab that can test it for iodine?" I asked. As a small animal nurse, she had never handled a pig sample before (apart from a guinea one), but, being an excellent nurse she took a deep breath and set about calling round some labs for me. Some semblance of normality returned when another old friend appeared, clutching a lamb with a broken leg. A late lambing ewe had delivered a lovely chunky lamb, even though it was now summer. But the lamb had had an accident and it's right fore leg flopped unnaturally. It was an easier fix than Hal and rounded off another interesting day in the life of a Yorkshire Vet.

Ticked Off

Even for a vet who thinks he has seen it all there are always surprises. In the middle of a full list of consultations, jam-packed with (what I'd call) normal jobs, one of the veterinary nurses thrust a dove in front of me.

"What do you think this is?" she asked. I moved my head back and moved the dove away – in the manner of anyone over the age of forty-five in need of an appointment with the opticians – so I could focus on the swollen thing attached to the dove, just above its right eye. I quickly decided it was a tick. I'd never seen a tick on a bird before and I thought they were solely a parasite of mammals with deer, hedgehogs, sheep, dogs and people being their standard targets. But apparently not. They can obviously attach to feathered surfaces too. The tick was swiftly removed and skewered on a hypodermic needle, to be displayed to anyone who wanted to see it, a bit like ruthless kings did with the heads of their enemies in times gone by. Of course, everyone wanted to peer at the horrible parasite because everyone dislikes ticks and nobody else had seen a tick on a bird before either.

It prompted an exchange other tick-type stories. There were various accounts of hedgehogs with too many ticks to count and a kitten with the pesky parasites that had become as fat and swollen as chickpeas. My favourite tick anecdote involved a worried lady who presented herself bashfully at the practice without an appointment one Saturday. She was very worried about a tick, just like the one above the dove's eye. After a brief introduction, the lady, without a dog on a lead or a cat in a basket, bent over, pulled down her trousers and displayed a large, engorged tick attached to her fleshy rump.

"Can you remove this for me, please?" came her strangled-sounding request as she doubled over.

Luckily for me, another nurse was on hand to do the deed and

another patient – albeit not a veterinary one – was cured. A human rather than an animal, but it didn't really matter. A tick is a tick in the end.

On the subject of humans seeking the help and advice of the vet, there was a concerned conversation on the phone recently. The elderly owner had, accidentally and inexplicably, taken her dachshund's heart medication tablets. Veterinary omni-competence can only go so far, and we quickly directed the unfortunate, and now light-headed owner, whose veins must have been dilating as we spoke, to the on-duty GP. Had it been the other way round, I would have been able to help. It is a common occurrence to get a panicked phone call to say that the dog has eaten the owner's tablets. The two favourites are ibuprofen – which is serious and necessitates instigation of emergency emesis to ensure the toxic drugs don't get absorbed – and contraceptive pills, which don't cause any harm to the dog but cause a lot of consternation to the owner. But while the effect of canine heart medication on a human was well out of my sphere of knowledge, I did need to add one thing,

"Once you're feeling better," I advised, "you should come and collect more tablets for the dog. It's really important she gets them all."

Luckily, all four individuals ended up fine: the dove flew away; the lady's rump was swiftly ticked off; the dachshund owner was absolutely fine; and the little sausage dog received a new supply of her canine medication.

Riding out of Quarantine

The boys and I were in mountain-biking action last weekend, at the UK's biggest mountain-biking event, the Ard Rock Enduro race in Reeth. The timing was perfect as we'd recently been honing our skills in Morzine – the Mecca of mountain-biking. The three of us had covered hundreds of kilometres of alpine trails, mostly at high speed.

The event in Swaledale was also perfect as it marked the end of our post-travel house arrest, the result of a last-minute and inexplicable rule change, just as we arrived in France. It was, at least, inexplicable to anyone with any geographical knowledge. Reportedly, the "beta variant" was running wild in France and there was concern from some that it might cross the channel and upset the perfectly implemented plans of virus control in the UK. In reality, some cases of this version of the virus had been detected on the small French island of La Réunion, which nestles safely and distantly between Madagascar and Mauritius, but the French include their overseas territories in their figures and this was the source of the apparent confusion. Up in the Alps, surrounded by fresh air and open space, we had a greater chance of meeting Heidi or Goat Peter on the alpine meadows than acquiring a mutant strain of COVID.

Luckily, we had built several layers of flexibility into our holiday, in case of such eventualities, so while the timing of changes was

A festival atmosphere in Reeth at the Ard Rock mountain-biking festival.

unfortunate, we all felt very lucky to have a holiday at all.

We sat out our house arrest diligently, testing ourselves as required and speaking to the friendly voices from Track and Trace, who phoned us three times a day. My jokes of "Oh, hello, is that the Gestapo again?" or "Ah, the Spanish Inquisition" were largely met with stony silence. So, in short, we were all pleased to be out of the house again and heading to the slopes of Swaledale – less huge than the alpine routes with which we had become acquainted, but no less intimidating. Friday was registration and practice day, followed by camping on site. Race day was Saturday. For downhill racing, practice is imperative – one mistake over choice of route could be, at best, detrimental to the timing or, at worst, downright dangerous.

Our excitement was rising as we drove over Grinton Moor, once made famous by the Tour de France (when it amusingly became known as Cote de Grinton Moor) and the tents, cars and bikes became visible in the valley below. It was shaping up to be a festival atmosphere as well as an excellent race. After registration, we scrutinised the maps and headed out. Enduro racing involves riding a loop with between three and seven specific timed downhill stages. The fastest aggregate downhill time wins. Whilst the whole route needs to be completed, in terms of the race it doesn't matter how quickly or slowly the uphill bits take. This didn't necessarily play into the hands of the fighting fit Norton household, freshly down from altitude, but it does make these events extremely inclusive as enthusiasts with all levels of fitness can participate. There were plenty of people pushing their bikes up the first stiff climb to the top of Fremington Edge.

At the top of stage one, we joined the queue for the first practice stage. It's impossible not to eye up the other bikes and riders; most of the bikes looked more fancy than ours and the riders – some internationally renowned and others fresh from Red Bull Hardline competition – were much more skilful. We took a deep breath and headed into the abyss.

Race Day

We'd enjoyed practice day on the steep slopes above Reeth, but race day on Saturday brought with it some nerves. The course was very challenging, with steep and muddy turns, off-camber descents and sharp and large rocks emerging from the track at all angles.

With a stiff wind and steady rain, we embarked on leg one. I set off last: we were all very aware that Dad was the slowest of the three Nortons. I didn't want to hold anyone up. It started well. The first two jumps safely negotiated, followed by a bomb hole, switchbacks, a loose, gravelly corner and some rocks. The adrenaline was bubbling like a geyser, until disaster struck. As I tried to make a crucial gear change before the next hard pedalling section – where I hoped to make up some time – my legs pedalled ten to the dozen but my speed fell to the point of grinding to a halt. My already glucose-deprived brain took moments to compute the problem. My chain had fallen off. In a stage race where seconds are crucial, to stop is bad enough but to have to perform essential maintenance work meant my chances of posting a respectable time had evaporated in the first section.

But never mind – I got it back on as swiftly as I could and pressed on, pushing hard. A big jump and some technical mud, rocks and turns in the woods at the bottom and even cheering from supporters with alpine cow bells and I re-joined the boys, who had been waiting patiently.

The rest of the ride was just as hard, with a minor crash and another mechanical incident. Aside from the racing, it was a joy to be out in the beauty of the Dales with my kids. As we climbed the final kilometres towards Reeth, over the heathery shoulder of Low Moor covered in regal purple, our legs were pumping and our lungs bursting with pure air. We were in our element. For me, it was a perfect day. It put me in mind of a bike adventure I had with my father, almost thirty-five years ago. On that day, we'd entered a sportive ride from Sheffield. It was sixty miles and included some of the behemoth climbs of the Peak District. Dad was keen because he could relive his university running days, when he'd pounded the same roads in trainers, decades before. In the 1980s, bikes came either from the tip and were fastidiously rebuilt, or handed down. The one Dad was riding was my grandfather's old track racing bike. Reliable (and successful) as it had been in its day, it was not very useful on the steep roads. With single speed and fixed gear, it was not possible to change gear or freewheel. Poor Dad struggled both on the climbs and the descents. I can't remember if I waited for him that day, but we both made it to the end. It was a tough ride, but I had the enthusiasm and fitness of youth – characteristics I recognised in abundance this weekend in the distant figures of my sons, as I toiled to try and keep up.

Back at the race headquarters in Reeth, we downloaded the information from the timing chips and scrutinised our times. The boys had done very well and anxiously waited to see if podium places would follow as more riders returned. As usual, my times were slowest and left me with a list of "what ifs" and "if only…" But unlike the day when *my* father was miles behind *me* in Derbyshire, I had few excuses and could certainly not blame the bike!

Descending to Reeth. Jack and Archie in the far distance.

Signing Contraband

I've been back on a book-signing circuit recently. My sixth book was out in the spring and so, as restrictions have relaxed, I've become reacquainted with the rigmarole of arranging and attending book-signings. When I was a novice to writing, I was encouraged by my first publisher to attend as many signings as humanly possible.

"It's great for sales!" the publicists shouted. At least, it is if people come to buy the books. It's not great for sales if you only sell four books. On many occasions, the meagre royalties would not even have covered the cost of the fuel in my car. Having subtracted the huge discounts, which the large book retailing chains demand, plus all the other stoppages, one feels great sympathy for proper authors who rely on their book sales to pay the mortgage. On one occasion, I travelled to the Wirral, enthusiastically following the M62 to a bookshop that was considered to be a Mecca for authors. I gave a talk, chatted with the owners, ogled over the signed pictures on the walls of Michael Palin, Rick Stein and Jeffrey Archer and then made my way home. As bad chance would have it, the M62 was closed that evening, apparently for essential maintenance, at three points on my return journey. The diversion signs were haphazard and my satnav, seemingly unfamiliar with the wrong side of the Pennines, did not help. I arrived home at half past three in the morning, more exhausted than if I'd been up all night at a calving. I'd sold about twenty books.

Nowadays I try to keep my travels more local. It can be hard to find the time, but it's really nice to meet people, lined up and clutching a book with my grinning face on it (I keep asking publishers to use a different type of front cover, but this never happens). Luckily, people who make the effort to travel to a bookshop at a specific time are pleased to see me, which doesn't always happen in real life. An anxious, cash-strapped farmer, preferably *doesn't* want to see me – his life is better if he doesn't need to meet a vet.

My first signing of the afternoon at a bookshop in Harrogate was for a lady who had come from almost as far away as the Wirral. She excitedly emptied contents of her bag onto the small table where I was sitting. It quickly became apparent that she had no intention of buying my new book, but wanted me to sign her hard-backed copies of my first two books.

"I don't think I can sign this," I said, as I inspected the second one. "It's a library book!"

"No, it isn't!" she exclaimed with indignation. "I bought it. From the internet."

I pointed out the obvious barcode on the spine, and the conspicuous plastic wrapper to protect it from wear and tear from (what should have been) borrowers, hungry to read veterinary stories. The library stamp on the title page made it unequivocally true. The book had clearly been stolen from a library and subsequently sold via an internet site! The lady from St Helens did not seem unduly perturbed by the dubious provenance of her book and so I felt obliged to add my signature to the contraband. After all, I knew what it was like to make a lengthy journey across the Pennines and I didn't want her journey to be totally in vain!

Admittedly, this was not the crime of the decade, but I felt sad because it had involved *my* book. I put my head down, added my signature along with Best Wishes, we chatted for a while and off she went, happy with her two signed copies.

Signings Round Two

After my encounter with a stolen book in Harrogate, the rest of the signing was uneventful. I met another lovely lady called Jane, who gave me a signed copy of *her* book, all about the Valley Gardens and how she and her friend had saved the horticultural delight from the worst fate a garden could be subjected to: being turned into a car park. She'd enlisted the help of various famous people to help her save the gardens, including the botanist David Bellamy and Alf Wight (which is why she thought I'd be interested). I confessed that I had never actually been to the Valley Gardens but promised I would make a visit a matter of priority.

I left Harrogate on time, which was important as I was heading all the way to Guisborough, which wasn't as nearby as I thought. Guisborough has a brilliant bookshop that always makes a huge effort and draws a crowd. I didn't expect people from Lancashire but I did expect lots of people. On my journey, I mulled over the question of the stolen book. It was hardly the most egregious of crimes, but it didn't seem right. Anne, my wife, is an avid book reader and thinks it is a crime to fold down corners of pages or bend the spine in the wrong manner, but those things don't bother me. Books are for reading and it doesn't matter if the pages are scuffed. It does matter though, if the thing's been stolen, because stealing it from a library prevents somebody else from reading it. It was like having your cake, eating most of it and then throwing the rest in the bin to stop others from enjoying the taste. I was not amused by someone's behaviour with my book.

Luckily, Guisborough Bookshop did not disappoint and there were plenty of people to cheer me up. The first time I visited was to deliver a talk in the town community building, which was called "Sunnyside". The name conjured up images of a retirement home, but it wasn't. It was a large, imposing stone building sitting, incongruously, in amongst the shops in the high street. It was a winter's evening and dark and there was a long queue extending out of the front doors. The preceding Zumba class had to clear up and wipe the sweat from the floor before we were allowed to enter. I remember being amazed that so many people had turned up because I was expecting an audience of about ten. I can't remember much about my talk that evening five and a half years ago, other than the fact that the projector wouldn't work, so I had to make it all up on the spot. It was chaos, but I think I got away with it.

Today, the queue was much shorter. Maybe the locals had grown fed up with books by local vets? Maybe visitors were outside enjoying the summer weather? But everyone was pleasant and the lady second or third in the queue, held out her book.

"It's nice to see you again, Julian," she smiled. "Please can you write 'To Jarred, enjoy your studies at Vet school', or something like that?" Then she added, "It's for my grandson. He came to see you at Sunnyside some years ago and from that evening on, he set his heart on being a vet. He's just about to start his first year at Liverpool."

It was the nicest thing that could have happened and amazing to have, in a small way, helped to shape the future for Jarred. It more than made up for my trauma of the book thief from Lancashire.

Alpaca Yoga?

It was a tempting offer, like nothing I'd ever had before. Perhaps I was looking stressed and in need of extra relaxation.

"I've started a yoga class. It happens in a field, with my alpacas," Jackie explained. "Would you like to come along? It's relaxing but also funny. Some of them try to join in!"

Certainly, there is an ethereal calmness that I have come to know around grazing alpacas, but coupling it with yoga? Could this be as close to nirvana as one could reach in North Yorkshire? Or would it all go wrong, with amusing antics and mischievousness to spoil the tranquillity? There was only one way to find out, and so on a sunny and pleasantly warm late summer evening, I found myself removing my shoes and socks and unrolling a yoga mat.

I was slightly late, having been held up by a Jack Russell holding his back leg off the ground at our practice in Thirsk. He really didn't want to be examined (how many Jack Russells do?) and so sedation was required to perform a proper job and work out what was going on. Luckily, the embedded thorn was easy to find and remove. I only missed the first few yoga moves, so I apologised and quickly took my place to join the class.

I'm not an expert on yoga, having been to just a handful of classes.

The first time was at university. A friend, Dave, and I thought the promised improvements in flexibility and core stability would be very helpful to our rock-climbing habit. Sadly, it didn't prove to be a great success as we both found ourselves snoring loudly at the end of the class, recumbent in the middle of the floor in a village hall on the outskirts of Cambridge. Today's yoga was definitely in a more pleasant setting. Insects buzzed and grass swayed in the warm breeze. Between the gentle instructions from our teacher, skylarks sang overhead as they bobbed higher and higher in the evening sky. The tranquillity and serenity were perfect – an idyllic environment to practise this ancient discipline. Maybe North Yorkshire was a good rival to the slopes of northern India, from where yoga originated? This *al fresco* yoga could catch on. But, despite the peace of nature, it was hard to achieve complete relaxation. I knew many of Jackie's alpacas quite well, having treated some – injections, examinations, castrations and caesarean sections – and delivered others into the world. The gang hovered close by, staring at our class.

"Why are those humans in our field, bending over and wobbling on one leg?" they must have been thinking. (I'm certain alpacas do a fair amount of thinking.) One of my patients, Julie, left the bunch and came over to say hello. I had delivered her by caesarean section and now she was almost a year old. Jackie had brought her up by offering her a bottle of special alpaca milk replacer every few hours during her formative weeks. Of course, she didn't recognise me, but she had become very bonded to humans, and indeed seemed to think of herself as one of us. So much so that she wanted to participate in the class. Julie went around and inspected everyone in turn, with a curiosity that only an inquisitive alpaca can have. Small squeaks or peeps were enough to confirm the pose was acceptable or otherwise. Relaxation slowly morphed into hilarity and the assembled group was soon chortling with laughter, as Julie was shortly followed by about six other alpacas joining in the class. As I tried to perfect my downward dog, right in front of me, and standing on my mat, was an upright alpaca.

Prolapsed Globe

The morning's ops list looked straightforward; a handful of dentals and some X-rays for a lame Labrador. It was busy enough but I hoped I'd have chance later to sort out some office work – I needed to chase up the delivery of orthopaedic equipment and two new computers needed to be unpacked, plugged in and installed. Not exactly life-saving veterinary work, but essential for the smooth running of our new practice in Thirsk. Six months in, we are very busy and finding time to do the routine administrative stuff is not always easy. A window of opportunity – an hour or so – after some routine ops, would need to be snapped up.

Of course, as usually happens, that window was slammed closed when an emergency call came in. Luckily, our nurse India does not deal in dramas and her consistently calm and collected manner kept our stress levels contained.

"There is a little puppy coming down. Her mum is really worried because her eyeball seems to have popped out," she explained. The popping out of an eyeball is a proper veterinary crisis and usually sends staff running in all directions. Experience is useful in these cases and we readied ourselves for action.

Sure enough Roonie, a little pug puppy, appeared with her right eye bulging and swollen like something from a horror film. The unfortunate pup had been playing with her brother and fallen down a step. The trauma had forced one of her already bulbous globes from its socket. Naturally, her devoted owner was devastated, fearing the worst. But we sprang into action.

"I'll take her straight to theatre," I blurted, grabbing the pug and whisking her away. It was a matter of great urgency. In critical cases like this, I always feel like I should apologise for not explaining in detail the plan and prognosis. But this could wait until later. My priority was to rescue the bulging and extruded eye.

Roonie was soon asleep, unconscious and therefore out of pain, at least for the time being. Replacing a prolapsed eye can be a bit like pulling on a pair of trousers which are really too tight. The globe quickly becomes swollen and also dried out on the surface, so plenty of lubrication and a procedure called a lateral canthotomy is required. This is where a small incision is made in the corner of the eye – to make the gap bigger – like moving the button on a pair of tight jeans. Next, special sutures are placed in each eyelid and a helpful nurse lifts the lids upwards. This allows the vet gently to apply pressure to the eyeball, returning it to its normal position. Because Roonie's owners had noticed the problem immediately, enabling us to get into action very quickly, the eyeball returned to its normal place relatively easily. Next, the lids needed to be sutured together to make sure the eyeball stayed in place and to protect the surface. It had gone very smoothly and, with plenty of analgesics on board, Roonie recovered in her kennel.

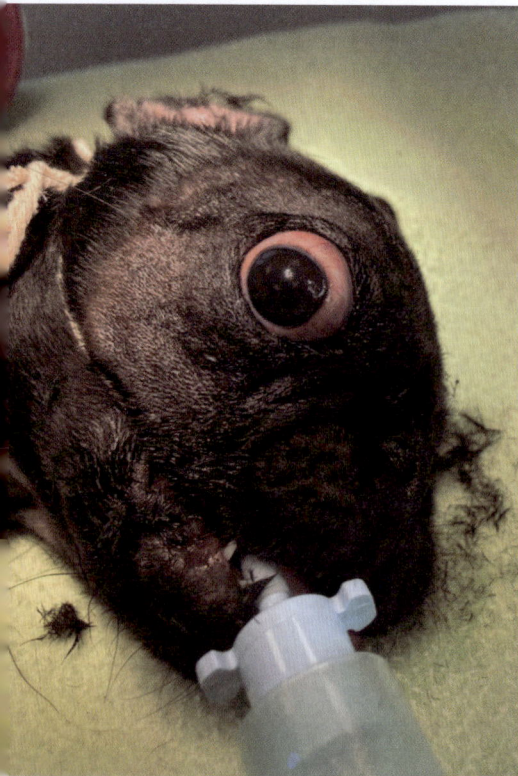

I made the call to her owners to confirm all had gone to plan. In many ways, this is one of the best bits of being a vet. Of course, the satisfaction of fixing a serious problem is something that is hard to beat, but relating the happy news of a successful surgery to an anxious owner is a highlight of any day. The puppy's owners were as delighted as I was. The real icing on the cake would be when they were finally reunited. But that was for later…

AOTF Horse Hoof

I was looking forward to meeting Jason and Ginger. Ginger was a horse and was lame, with sore feet and wonky legs. Jason was an experienced farrier, skilled and adept at scrutinising X-rays, analysing gait and working out what to do next.

I've treated lots of horses over my veterinary career, but I don't have much experience in the field of corrective farriery. I hoped Jason would pass on some of his knowledge during my time with him and Ginger. I would ask interesting and incisive questions as two cameras captured all the action. At least, that was the plan.

Jason, Ginger and I were to be part of a VT about the work of skilled farriers for the series *Autumn on the Farm* – a spin-off from Channel 5's *Springtime on the Farm* that began back in 2016 – which started last week. My role was not really as a vet, but as an interested and slightly knowledgeable interlocutor; and I was excited to be involved. I'd spoken with Jason the previous day, to discuss the case and explain what would be involved. Early on a Sunday, he was happy to chat and his boundless enthusiasm boomed down my phone. I couldn't wait to meet him and learn about his work. Of course, Jason didn't disappoint. He was born and bred with horses and had worked with them for most of his life. "If I'm honest, I prefer

horses to people," he confided shortly after we met, on a lovely livery just outside Harrogate.

Then we met Ginger. I confessed to Jason that it had been a while since I'd scrutinised the nuances of the lower limb of an equine. Politely, he explained the wonky angles, laterally displaced joints, pigeon toes and boxy hooves, while Zara and Jacob focused and pull-focused from all angles with their cameras. Everything was captured on film, but it was a normal and natural conversation and I hung on Jason's every word of wisdom.

Navicular disease or, more accurately, navicular syndrome was to blame. The pressure from flexor tendons on an important bone in the hoof was either the cause or the consequence of the abnormal lower limb conformation and we watched the effect of this as Ginger stood, then walked and finally (with coercion) trotted up. And then the work began: trimming, paring, dressing and rebalancing the foot using knives and rasps. Within minutes, the hoof was much more shapely. Next was the new shoe. Bespoke and perfectly sculptured for the foot, the shoe fitted as snuggly as Cinderella's. Next (inserted between the shoe and sole) came soft, cushioning plastic wedges, to raise the heel and remove pressure from the digital flexor tendons. The stressed navicular bone would surely soon feel more comfortable. I watched and imagined the relief, similar to wearing heel wedges in running shoes to ease an injured Achilles tendon. Ginger behaved impeccably, as if he knew that Jason was helping and appreciated his caring attention. The final pièce de resistance was the insertion of a cushioning gel, squirted in via a special gun. It was amber and clear with flashy silvery bits and suffused the surface of the sole, filling the gap and offering extra soft cushioning. It looked comfy and snazzy.

As we let the gluey gel set and trotted Ginger up and down to see how much he had improved, I thanked Jason for the fascinating insight into his specialist world.

"I wish I'd met you twenty-five years ago," I confessed, "when I was just starting out as a vet. You might just have changed my career!"

Llama Jaw

A fraught message about an injured llama had me dropping everything and rushing over to Nidderdale. Suzanne was worried about Rowan, one of her youngsters, who had suddenly stopped being able to eat. Food was spilling from his mouth along with drool and blood. Something was obviously seriously wrong and I arranged to go and visit as soon as I could. We were anxious that the jaw might be fractured.

The drive along the banks of the Nidd gave me time to recollect a similar llama drama, about five years ago. A huge and handsome boy called Dobbie had been injured and I can recall the case with clarity. The suspicion was that Dobbie had been kicked in the head. His sad, floppy and asymmetric face had a long stream of bloody saliva dripping steadily onto the straw. Laura, my PD (producer-director) had travelled with me that day, pointing her camera from the passenger seat of my car and interviewing me all the way. I stared at Dobbie and she stared at me, Laura's camera poised. "What are you going to do, Julian?" she asked, probing for a decisive plan or an answer that might build jeopardy.

But there was already plenty of jeopardy. Dobbie clearly had a broken jaw and I had to work out a plan to repair it. If I couldn't, he would need to be put down, which wasn't a palatable option. I peered inside his mouth and then started to ponder. But beyond ponder, I needed to do something and this wasn't in the veterinary text books. I decided to try to lasso the loose jaw fragments with strong nylon sutures, to act like a set of braces that a child with wonky teeth might wear. It seemed to work and Dobbie's mouth started to look much more normal. Moments later, he shoved his head into the hay net and started munching with miraculous abandon.

Dobbie recovered well and is still an important and senior member of the herd. I often think about that successful day, with a delighted owner, a cured patient and an unusual and popular story for my television series. If Rowan had a broken jaw as well, at least I could tap into previous experience. This time (and with the benefit of that experience) I had prepared myself with more appropriate surgical tackle. Orthopaedic wire, cutters and twisters and a small hand-drill in case I needed to drill a hole in the jaw. I had no X-ray facilities, but I hoped a clinical examination would suffice to provide the diagnosis.

The other difference was that, this time, I had no PD riding shotgun, but I'd messaged Ross (my current cameraman) who arranged to meet me at Suzanne's to capture the action, should there be any. I've worked hard on *The Yorkshire Vet* over the last six years and we've managed to capture and share hundreds of stories of veterinary action during this exciting period of my career. Obviously, we need the cases and also the cooperation and compliance of veterinary staff and clients. Without them and their enthusiastic assistance, we have no programme and so everyone involved with production is endlessly grateful for this. It's also imperative that there is always someone nearby with a camera, so the action can be captured. It's tough for the camera team, who have to juggle things constantly to try to cover veterinary action from the Pennines to the Dales and now the North Yorkshire Moors. It's hard to keep all the plates spinning and I was delighted Ross could drop everything and come to film Rowan this evening. He was there when I arrived. I just hoped I could help…

Awards and More Awards

Attending an awards ceremony can be more exciting than Christmas. Dressing up smartly, chatting to old and new friends and enjoying lovely food and good wine is a real highlight. One of the best I have been to, was the National Television Awards, several years ago. I chatted with members of *Gogglebox*, stood at the urinals next to David Jason and held Johnny Vegas's pint whilst he lit another cigarette. But not all awards evenings are as heady as that and there have been occasions, I have to admit, where the evening has not been so wild.

But after the horrors of Covid, there is a pent-up excitement: the atmosphere of these events this autumn promises to be as effervescent as the bottles of bubbly that the winners will no doubt be opening late into the night. I dusted off my DJ for a biggie: The Royal Television Society Yorkshire awards, for which *This Week on the Farm* was nominated. I have had only a peripheral role in this popular series, but Anne and I had kindly been invited along. Ben Frow, Channel 5 controller and honorary Yorkshireman, was also coming and I was keen to catch up. Ben has done more for the Yorkshire tourist industry than pretty much anyone else, commissioning series like *Our Yorkshire Farm*, *This Week on the Farm*, the risky-but-super-successful remake of *All Creatures Great and Small* and, of course, *The Yorkshire Vet*. I really hoped we'd be sitting with him, because a rumour was about that he was up for a special award! I could relax and enjoy the event, for there was no chance I'd have to go up on stage. The last time I'd been to the RTS I had to receive a trophy and, in optimistic anticipation, I tried to limit the wine consumption. I did, but my few words of acceptance were slurred with emotion. I was happy I wouldn't have to do it again.

The night lived up to expectations. Ben was visibly moved by the recognition by the RTS for both his huge contribution to telly and especially to our county. For Ben, surely bigger honours await.

One week on and the hangovers had subsided. The DJ was out again. It was the Yorkshire Post Rural awards, an old favourite of Anne and mine. We've spent several pleasant evenings enjoying funny anecdotes and convivial company (we always seem to end up next to Harry Gration) as well as handing out the occasional award. Tonight though, we were up for our own award. Thirsk Veterinary Centre, only six months into its new life, was on the list of finalists. We've worked incredibly hard – especially Anne and Isabella who are the main protagonists at the new practice – and it's fair to say our first half a year has exceeded what we had hoped, with almost two thousand new clients already. How the candidates for Rural Business and Professional Services would be ranked and assessed was anyone's guess, but I gave my shoes an extra polish before we left, just in case. Naturally, I'd eyed up the competition in advance, which looked tough; a chainsaw business and a company that trains people in important rural skills such as crop spraying.

Our small team is built up of old and new friends and former colleagues. Cathy, our receptionist, and I started our careers in veterinary practice in Thirsk on the same day, more than twenty-five years ago. We share some funny memories and have had many a night out, but we'd never been to an awards ceremony together. But there we all were, smartly dressed in evening dresses and bow ties rather than scrub suits or operating gowns and everyone was excited.

The shortlist was announced, and then, "and the winner is…"

Suspicious, but Life-Saving Liquids

There was no possibility of taking the bottles through security – of that, I was certain. Two 500ml plastic bottles, each containing clear, amber liquid were sure to arouse suspicion. This was one of the reasons I was fidgeting uncomfortably as I waited in the queue for the security checks. Another was that I was not accustomed to wearing a suit and a neat tie with its knot thrust firmly against my throat. A third was that my imminent appointment was with royalty!

I had been invited to Kensington Palace, to a reception in support of the Cheetah Conservation Fund (CCF) UK, a charity for which I have recently become an ambassador. Princess Michael of Kent is the royal patron and was the host this sunny afternoon. I was excited to have the chance to meet her and learn more about the work of the CCF in saving this most amazing animal. Royal security protocols would surely not allow my peculiar liquids into a palace.

Two days earlier, I'd had a message from someone at the charity. Their vet from Somaliland had arrived. Laurie looked after baby cheetahs which were ill. She was also in charge of the livestock-guarding dog programme, which has been so successful in reducing cheetah–human conflict. Farmers are given Anatolian dogs, which live with their goats to warn away predators such as cheetahs. Loss of habitat has forced wild animals into much closer contact with humans in recent decades, but keeping one of these dogs with the herd means the cheetahs steer clear of livestock – so they are less likely to be shot by farmers.

Laurie was desperate for some vitamin injections for the sick cheetah cubs under her care and this was what the message had been about. I promised to try and find some, although I feared that particular solution of vitamins and amino acids had been discontinued. Certainly, I hadn't seen any for many years. Back in the day, the amber elixir was used in any circumstance where a boost was required or if a diagnosis was inconclusive. Old vets would inject big syringes into the drip bags of any poorly patient. Ironically, the resulting yellow liquid infusion was often dripped intravenously into jaundiced dogs and cats, as if fighting yellow with yellow. (Is this homeopathy?)

On one fateful occasion, late at night and many years ago, a tired and short-sighted senior vet set up a drip for a sick Dobermann. It was golden yellow and he presumed it was the marvellous vitamin mix. But (so the story goes) in his nocturnal daze, he hadn't read the label and the dog benefitted from a slow intravenous infusion of dilute iodine solution! Luckily, there were no ill-effects and the dog's internal organs were thoroughly cleansed. Whilst this was a grave error and obviously never to be recommended, the results were surprisingly favourable.

After a bit of searching, I managed to find a supplier and ordered a couple of bottles, which I stowed in my bag. I didn't know how I was going to convince the security people of my story. Luckily, just in time, Laurie appeared. We spoke for a while about our common interests and I gleaned information hungrily from this enthusiast. Then finally I got chance to open my bag.

"I've got you a present, Laurie. It's for your cheetah cubs. I didn't think this was still available, but these two bottles should help." With a grin all over her face, Laurie held the prized bottles aloft, just like baby Simba in the *Lion King*. My mission was accomplished!

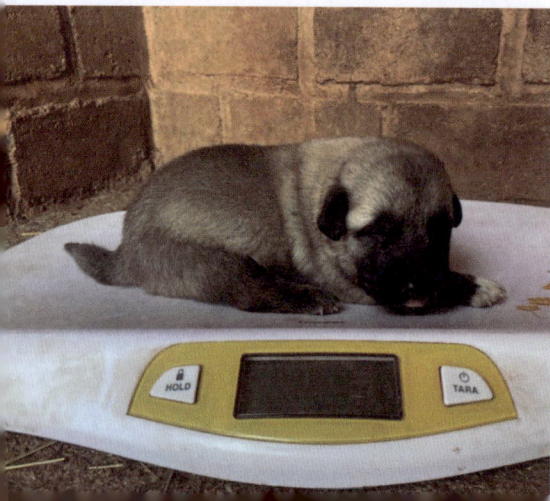

A puppy Anatolian Shepherd dog gets weighed in, ready for action to help save the cheetah.

Two Practices

Being involved and closely connected with two practices is really great. Watching the growth of two nascent businesses is like nurturing two small children. Each day, new challenges appear and small hurdles are overcome. An extra vet is employed; a new trainee veterinary nurse is welcomed into the team. Another new hope is ignited and another Government Gateway (to sign up another apprenticeship) is navigated. Happy new clients register and, at Thirsk, old friends and previous patients appear through the waiting room door daily. I met one recently, a Labrador called Hailey. Now she is ten, and aging gracefully. I'd seen her as a puppy and (eventually) diagnosed an unusual case of a gallstone in young middle age. That day, many years earlier, her owner, delighted when a concrete diagnosis had finally been made, hugged me firmly and gratefully in the dimmed lights of an X-ray room. I hadn't forgotten her emotion on that day.

And we are sharing the joy of seeing new businesses develop. Younger partners, at both Wetherby and Thirsk practices, take on a big role, but with some support from more senior vets. Mark, Anne and I (the old vets) can pass on wisdom and knowledge, as well as continuing to work hard at the coalface. Isabella and Helen can either judiciously ignore us or take confidence from experience based on previously negotiated problems. It's working well. For my part, I'm the only one working in both places and it does sometimes scramble my tired brain.

"Hello, Sandbeck Veterinary Centre," I enthusiastically bellowed down the phone at Thirsk yesterday. Nurses in the background laughed and waved their hands vigorously sideways to remind me I'd got it wrong. On a morning, I have to screw up my forehead at the junction in Sowerby. "Is it left or right today?" I ask myself. But despite the minor confusions, I'm loving my dual veterinary life. I get the best of both worlds and, as I've got very used to over recent years, I'm tackling two jobs at the same time.

The two new practices share equipment and borrow drugs. Orthopaedic drills, saws, pins and screws accompany me back and forth most days. And there is often a packet or more of medication to transfer from one surgery to another. I sometimes think, if only I could attach some kind of road sweeper to my car I could sweep the A1 twice a day as well!

Last week, I swapped a much sought-after vaccine from one practice to the other. It was a drug in short supply across the country and an expectant Labrador was in need of a dose to safeguard her pregnancy. The vaccine would prevent a nasty disease caused by herpes virus and, for bitches requiring this cover, it is crucial. Like many essential products in the post- COVID, post-Brexit Armageddon, the supply is erratic and woefully inadequate (has anything improved after Brexit?). Luckily, there were a few spare doses in the fridge at Sandbeck. One of them could easily be spared for a very grateful client at Thirsk.

Also with luck, I'd remembered the tonometer (an expensive piece of kit for measuring the pressure inside an eye) along with the herpes vaccine. I brandished the vial above my head as soon as I arrived, announcing the arrival of the crucial vaccine, before placing it safely in the fridge.

Moments later, I overheard a conversation between a nurse and Isabella, which I found funny. It was both worrying and reassuring at the same time and uttered without any trace of comedy.

"Julian has the tonometer. And he's brought Herpes from Wetherby."

If anyone in the waiting room had overheard the comment, I felt certain there would be no hugs for me today, no matter how grateful the owner!

Skewered

Dogs in Yorkshire have been swallowing some strange things over the last few weeks. Rocco, the young Rhodesian ridgeback, was a typical case. The youngster, normally with unwavering enthusiasm and a vigorous lust for life, was being sick and looking uncharacteristically lacklustre. It was the time for some X-rays.

But I suspected the cause as soon as the image appeared on the screen, because I'd seen the suspicious signs many times before. "I reckon it's a corn-on-the-cob," I declared confidently. Minutes later, after phone calls had been made, anaesthetics administered and an abdomen prepared, I was peering inside the dog's abdomen, where a very obvious foreign body was lodged stubbornly in the intestines. Corn-on-the-cob can do extraordinary damage to the small intestine, where it becomes completely jammed like a cork. The intestine tries its best to push it along but ends up stretched and devitalised, sometimes to the point that large sections have to be removed. Fortunately, in this case the tissue was still reasonably healthy and, before long, I was watching Rocco recover in his kennel. He'd been lucky and would make a full recovery.

But, as dramatic as Rocco's corn was, another patient won the prize for top foreign body. The spaniel had visited several vets around Yorkshire to try and solve his malaise, all to no avail. His owners arrived at Sandbeck, desperate for help. The lump on his side, recently identified as a benign and incidental fatty lump, turned out to be anything but. Poor old Charlie was in great pain and feeling awful. It was our new vet Ed's turn to come to the rescue. Ed saw practice with me as a student about five years ago. He shone as an unassuming but confident, pleasant and capable student with great potential. I'd kept in contact, knowing he'd make a great addition to our team at some point and this has indeed turned out to be the case.

More X-rays were taken, and heads were scratched. I had the

nagging feeling we could be dealing with another gastric foreign body.

Brows were furrowed and eyebrows raised, but the more I thought about it, the more I felt confident I was on the right track and persuaded Ed to reach for his scalpel. I'd seen this sort of thing before. An accidentally ingested and pointy foreign body, like a kebab stick from a barbecue, can perforate the stomach wall and make a slow and steady bid to escape through the body wall, impossible to find until it finally pokes up under the skin somewhere.

"Make an incision over that swollen bit, Ed," I advised. "Dissect down and see what you find. My bet is that it'll be a wooden skewer."

Ed made tentative cuts, exploring methodically and cautiously. Suddenly, and without warning, he announced, "Oooh. I can feel something."

"What can you feel?" I asked, eager to find out more.

"Something spikey," he explained succinctly, after a dramatic pause, matter-of-factly but with just enough jeopardy to keep everyone in attendance enthralled. We held our collective breaths and watched with excitement. The spikey something was grasped with forceps and Ed, like King Arthur withdrawing Excalibur from its stubborn home in a rock, slowly but very deliberately removed a six-inch wooden skewer from the swelling. It was dramatic and a bit gruesome, but would prove to be totally curative. To Charlie's owners (especially once they'd seen the video) Ed, quite rightly, had acquired legendary status. Rocco's owners, in the meantime, had realised their own dog was also rapidly becoming a veterinary legend, for all the wrong reasons. He was back just two days after his sutures had been removed. He'd swallowed another corn cob!

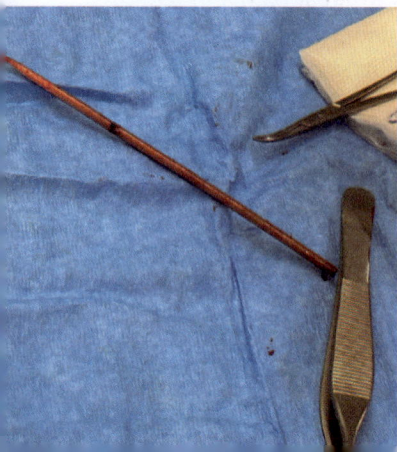

A pesky wooden skewer.

Foraging

I've been foraging this week, under the supervision of Craig who is an expert on finding food in the wild. It's something I've been interested in since a kid; I'm sure the instinct to collect food from nature, whenever it is plentiful, is innate. I can recall autumnal blackberry-picking excursions with my gran when I was a small boy. We'd try to out-do one another and fill our plastic tubs to the brim. The result, later in the day, was always a pie, crusty and sweet with intensely flavoured juices escaping from any holes and eaten straight from the enamel pie dish. Sometimes apples were involved.

I hoped Craig would take me from blackberries and apples – both identifiable by anyone – to the exciting but potential deadly world of mushrooms. The purpose of the day was to film a piece for a new television series with which I am involved. It may be secret at the moment, so I probably shouldn't spill any beans. I met Craig and he handed me a wicker basket. I hoped I'd be filling it with wild produce and not spilling any of that either. With his dreadlocks and long, wooden staff, he was the very epitome of a woodsman. I quickly realised he was as knowledgeable as he was enthusiastic as he swooped in on some sorrel. Nestling amongst nettles, the bright and shiny leaves looked a bit like basil and we plucked some for our lunch. But leaves alone would not satisfy our appetites. What we really wanted were some

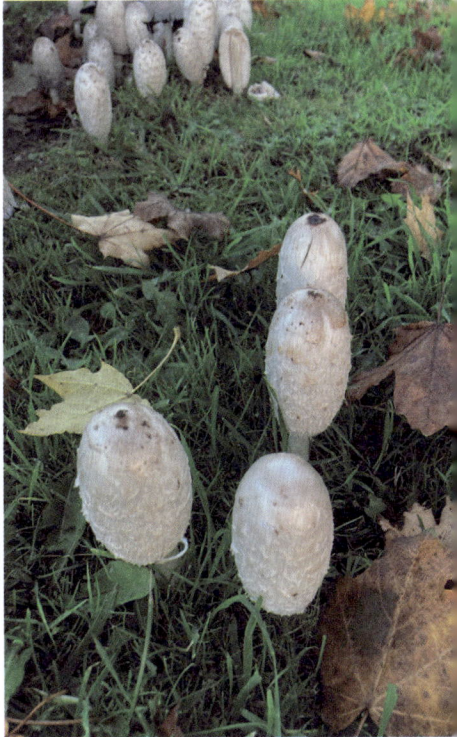

Shaggy Ink Caps? I hope so!

mushrooms. Craig pointed his stick in the direction of a corner of the wood full of pine trees, declaring, "I think there might be some porcini mushrooms over there." Porcini is the Italian word for this fungus, literally meaning "little pig". In England, they are called a cep, or a penny-bun (big ones have a top which looks like a bread bun).

It didn't take long before Craig beckoned me over to where he was crouching under the trees. Sure enough, we'd got ourselves a cep. It was small, but quite well formed. "And you're *definitely* certain it's not poisonous," I asked as he sliced a sliver for me to sample. It tasted delicious. With food miles of approximately thirty centimetres, it was a mini-meal with no impact on the planet. Already, I was hooked on foraging and wandered off, eyes down in search of more. Moments later, I'd found another tree with more ceps popping out from amongst the fallen leaves at its foot. Our baskets were filling fast, but Craig explained that the motto of the forager must always be to "just take enough" and to "leave some for others, including the wildlife". It was a far cry from the panic-grabbing we've seen over the last year or so, first with toilet roll, then with food and more recently with fuel.

Back in the kitchen, the mushroom risotto, laced with previously collected dried mushrooms and chanterelle powder, was one of the most mushroom-intense meals I've ever eaten. The only ingredients not from within five miles were the rice and the olive oil.

The next morning, whilst walking Emmy, I struck gold again. A patch of gloriously firm, pale golden 'shrooms. I didn't know what they were, but they looked tasty and I resolved to get a book, identify them then hopefully collect some for my tea.

They looked like "Shaggy Ink Caps". In my new book, there was a smiley face next to them, so I picked a few, feeling reasonably confident I'd got it right. If there is no *Yorkshire Vet* column next week, you'll know I've made a huge mistake…

Foraging Again and a Pig

I scrutinised in detail the pages of *Mushrooms and Toadstools of Britain and Europe*, to check and double-check those I had found on my dog walk. I was about 90% certain they matched the description of the "Shaggy Ink Cap". I uprooted a few and put them in my bag, ensuring I left sufficient for nature (or other foragers) to enjoy. Craig, my fun, fungi guy, had insisted upon two things: "only take what you need" and "if in doubt, leave it out". But did 90% certainty constitute a credible amount of "doubt"? In my mind, not at all. So, with great excitement, I sliced some portions when I got home and offered them to Archie, my raw-mushroom eating son. Of course, I tested some on myself first. Two minutes after the mushroom, I was still alive and sentient, without any trace of illness and with no obvious hallucinations. Archie, soon after eating, was also fine. Or so it seemed.

Later that evening we were all in the car on the way for a family meal. It had been another busy Saturday, starting before six for Archie to get to his swim training. You don't get to be Yorkshire Champion by having a lie-in on a morning. After that, I'd been to do morning surgery, followed by a session signing books at White Rose Book Café in Thirsk in the afternoon. We were all looking forward to a convivial evening after a long day. In the darkness of a late autumn evening, the back seat of the car was dark and soon silent. Archie was slumped, unresponsive and unmoving. "Is he dead?" asked Anne, who had been sceptical of my mushroom adventure from the start.

"I hope not," was all I could add, followed by, "Well, I feel OK." Luckily for Archie, he was simply catching up on missed sleep and hadn't been accidentally poisoned by his father. This was also lucky for me, as marital harmony was maintained. My first, unsupported fungal foray had ended happily as well as tastily!

Later that week, veterinary work had me doing something else for the first time. I'd last seen this patient almost a year earlier, when I'd castrated him as a noisy piglet. He'd visited me at the practice when he was just a few weeks old. I'd followed his progress as a proper pet pig over the year and so I was worried when his owner phoned me in a panic. Pigley had been trodden on by one of the horses. Since I knew he spent most of his day sleeping by the Aga, my first thought was, "Why was there a horse in the kitchen?" But this was not a laughing matter, because the hoof on one of his trotters had been ripped off and blood was everywhere. Now fully-grown, Pigley could definitely not be transported to the practice, like a dog with a broken nail. The pig was too big. It was my turn to visit him.

I gathered what I thought I'd need and headed out on a pig visit that was sure to be very different to the usual visit a pig vet might expect. Pigley was lying in his bed in the kitchen. I have learnt that *stealth* is the best approach to persuading a pig to cooperate, and I applied this by the bucketful. With soothing, encouraging and calming words from everyone nearby, I soon had the injured foot cleaned and wrapped in a bandage, securely strapped on. There was only minor grumbling and occasional grunts from the patient. A pig examined and treated in a kitchen and my first foray into mushroom picking: both had been a success!

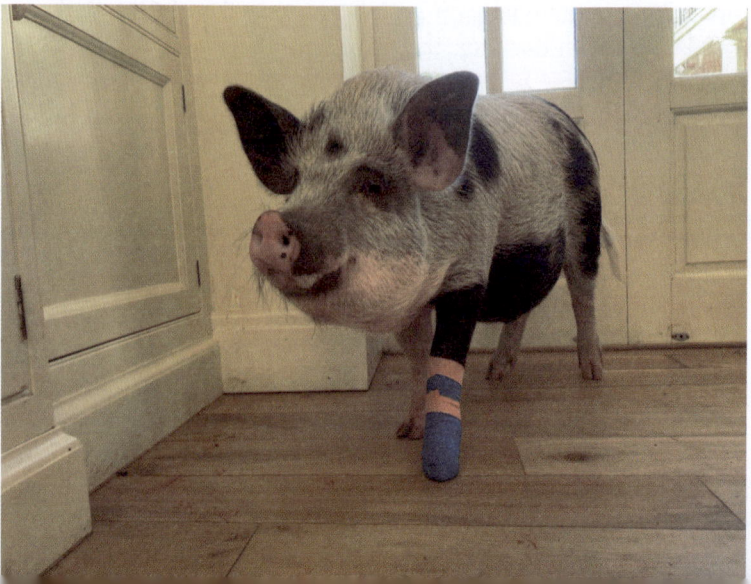

Little Dead Cat

I've been catching up with lots of old farmer friends recently. Our new practice in Thirsk is situated at the Rural Business Centre and Auction Mart, so I see farmers every Thursday as they queue up to sell cattle and sheep. Or, more frequently, as they queue up to buy pie and mash for dinner at the cafe next door. Some look older, shorter, or more lame, but most look just the same. Some carry on as they have done for decades; some have retired, but can't give up the habits of a lifetime and still come down to the auction mart each week. One farmer, Richard, who I've known for over twenty-five years has been into the practice a few times recently. In the past, I have delivered lambs and calved cows for him, at weekends, in the evenings and late at night. I've done his TB test countless times and dehorned and disbudded calves each autumn after housing. And I've treated many of his army of cats, each one just as precious to him as any ewe.

I saw his name on my list of appointments. Next to his name it said *Little Dead Cat. Second opinion.*

"What's this cat all about?" I asked Sue, our receptionist-cum-admin guru. "I'm a good vet, but I'm not that good. I don't think I can help a little cat which is already dead!"

"I think that's its name," Sue explained.

I decided, for the avoidance of confusion, to simplify the cat's name on our computer records to "L.D.C". I called Richard in, and wasted no time catching up on the trials and tribulations and changes of circumstances since we'd last seen each other, which I think was at about two o'clock in the morning on a cold night in winter; I'd calved his favourite cow. Eventually, we turned our attention to the contents of the cat box.

"So, this little cat. It's not actually dead is it?" I asked. "If so, there's not much I can do for it, I'm afraid."

Richard smiled quietly and explained that she had been given that name shortly after she was born, many years previously, because she was little and so weak. She was presumed to be dead. A neonatal miracle unfolded and the little dead cat survived, but the name stuck, as the pragmatic farmer had seen no need to alter it.

This morning, the now elderly tortoiseshell was anything but dead. But there was a challenging, smelly and infected problem with her ear, which is why the farmer wanted another set of eyes to make an assessment. The first vet he'd seen had offered a grave prognosis and recommended immediate euthanasia. Once upon a time, it was very unusual for clients to ask for a second veterinary opinion from another practice. Now it is quite common and clients often move and change vets depending on the differential levels of ability, skills and experience available.

I could see some hope though, and knew that having survived being "dead" in the first few hours of life, L.D.C. was strong. I offered some trial treatment, in reality it would probably be mainly palliative, but everyone (including the cat) wanted to try something. A week later, L.D.C was back for a check-up. The nasty infected smell had disappeared, the discharge abated and L.D.C. had started eating again. "*L.D.C., V.M.B*", I typed on the clinical notes, *VMB* standing for "very much better".

Richard headed back to the Land Rover clutching his cat basket, but before he left for his farm, he couldn't resist popping into the mart for a quick catch-up and a chat. Old habits die hard. Old cats, of course, do die, but thankfully not today.

The Lights Are On

I've been feeling a bit gloomy recently. This is mainly because of the big reduction in time spent outside and on my mountain bike. Two things have conspired: my mountain-biking soulmate, aka my eldest son Jack, has left for university, so I'm short of convenient biking friends and, just as bad, the onset of dark nights has truncated the daytime and dramatically reduced the chances of getting out on the hills.

My part of North Yorkshire has some of the best mountain-biking anywhere. There is an almost unbroken escarpment of steep slopes from Carlton Bank at the north to beyond Kilburn further south, with lovely, well-draining ground and a mix of open moors and woodland. And there's a treasure-trove of trails on the moors and in the dales if you are ready to explore. For mountain-biking, North Yorkshire could rival the Alps, Innerleithen in the Scottish Borders, Utah in the US and the coastal hills of northern Italy. What's required is a joined-up strategy involving landowners, riders and forestry people to develop the area into something really amazing. It could be the ultimate in diversification, encouraging people out to enjoy the countryside and fresh air of Yorkshire, with cafes for hungry riders, bunk houses to stay in, riding passes for acccss, bike shops and more. The possibilities, I think, are endless and would offer an easier and sustainable income from land that is often barely profitable by conventional farming methods.

But much as this might be a brilliant plan for the future, it didn't solve my immediate problems. What did help was a new set of night lights, so I could ride after dark! Last time I went proper mountain-biking in the dark was over twenty years ago, when I was younger and fitter and with more acute eyesight, but also when batteries were huge, rubbish and short-lived. As large as an oil barrel, but as temporary as a snowman in November, the energy source would quickly dwindle and the brightness dim to a dangerously dark level. Rides had to have a back-up plan and were not really much fun. Nowadays, there is much more power in a rechargeable battery!

I set off, sensibly (I thought) in the dusk of a November Sunday. Other riders and even dog walkers, were already packing up as I arrived in the car park, unloaded the bike and prepared my equipment. The woods looked beautiful in the late autumn twilight, with gold and orange shades everywhere. The first couple of runs were in daylight and covered in crispy dry fallen leaves rather than mud. The trails were as exciting as I'd expected, but before my third descent, darkness fell leaving me to test out the lumens of my torch, calculate the optimal descending speed under the new circumstances and take in the crepuscular wildlife.

The power of the lights proved to be amazing, illuminating everything in my path like a beam from a lighthouse. It was exhilarating too and also other-worldly. With the senses heightened, even at sensible speeds the excursion was epic. And as for the wildlife! With owls hooting, foxes scuttling across the path and a couple of deer, skipping over a silvery stream, my evening could have been taken from the scenes in a children's book. I felt privileged to have been part of the woodland night.

My evening adventure had been super and I'd loved every minute. Lots of people might think this sort of thing is crazy, dangerous and only for lunatics. I can confirm for certain, that the lights were on and I was *definitely* at home!

Packet of Biscuits

Friday was a day full of spaniels. I've got no idea why, but we had eleven in total, waiting in and passing through the waiting room. Admittedly, four of them were littermates and just eight weeks old, but there were eight appointment slots filled with the cheerful, bushy-eared breed, of both the cocker and springer variety. Last week, we had an influx of Yorkshire terriers, with five in the practice at the same time on one day. Nobody knows why these things happen. It's the same unknown phenomenon of busy versus quiet nights on call. I once had a colleague who always swore a swapped weekend on duty would lead to one that was excessively busy. I never was afflicted by the curse of a ridiculously hectic swapped weekend, but I've had my fair share of busy on-calls. I can remember a Saturday afternoon and evening in which I undertook four bitch caesarean sections – more than the practice would usually do in as many weeks. I'd literally just get home, put the kettle on and the beeper would go off again. Another time, between the hours of two and six on a Monday morning, I had three separate uterine prolapses in three different cows, on three different farms – one of the most messy and challenging jobs for any vet. That night, instead of the kettle and a cup of tea, it was sleep of which I was repeatedly deprived.

I'd had my hands full with the series of spaniels

and had only popped my head into the prep room and theatre to check that everyone was OK and that the ops list was in order. It was busy back there, too, but Ed was totally in control. I left him to it and didn't interfere or scrutinise the patients, other than to offer some advice on a couple of X-rays and an ultrasound scan image. This is one of the brilliant benefits of practices like ours. There's always a more senior vet around to help and give support when required. Or, occasionally, to be ignored if the advice is out-dated and irrelevant (this is rare). It's the way veterinary practices always used to function and having another opinion, or another set of eyes, or another experienced pair of fingers to palpate an abdomen is hugely helpful. Even with a combined total of over sixty years of practice under our belts, Helen, Mark and I confer most days over clinical cases and decision-making.

We also have an excellent system, designed by Lucy our head nurse. Each hospitalised patient has a small, plastic box assigned to it. Prior to its op, the catheter, medicines and other accoutrements are placed inside. The patient's name is written on the side, in wipe-clean felt tip pen, so the name can be changed each day. Post-op discharge sheets, medicines, samples in formalin pots or blood tubes are also put inside so they are neat and organised and nothing gets lost. It works very well. I cast an eye over the boxes and was surprised to see that there was another coincidence of seismic proportions affecting our practice. One plastic box had "Biscuit – Lhasa Apso" written on the side. An adjacent box had the words: "Biscuit – Labrador". We had two dogs in with the same name! And an unusual one at that. A pair of "Rockys", "Brackens", "Milos", "Defors" or "Maxs" would not have been unusual, but I couldn't remember the last time I'd seen a Biscuit at a vets. At least not one with hair and four legs.

"How strange!" I exclaimed, pointing at the biscuit boxes. "We almost have a packet of biscuits!" Lucy, once again, rolled her eyes at another terrible joke.

Snowy Vet Days

The recent snowy spell has led me to reminisce about some of the freezing winters I've endured during my life as a vet. Foggy, dark and damp days set in from around the middle of October in Thirsk, and from the end of November no one is totally surprised to see snow.

I used to do the annual pregnancy testing visit to a large suckler herd near Nether Silton every November. It was a wild job and took several days. We would start work at about nine in the morning and finish whenever darkness fell. It took ages, because the cattle were out in the field and didn't want to be captured and separated from their calves. Once tested, they were ferried to one farm or another, depending on the outcome of the test. If we were lucky, the work would be done in two days and completed without any injuries or escapees. We were also lucky if we didn't get snow falling at some stage. If the wind came from the north, then it was a near certainty. The only part of my body that remained warm was my right arm. Every few minutes it would be immersed in a rectum at just over one hundred and one degrees Fahrenheit. It was like submerging it in a lovely warm bath. Sadly, the same could not be said for my feet – wellies and frozen concrete are not a good combination. My left hand was not as fortunate as the right. It grappled with the freezing cold metal workings of the cattle crush, sucking out any warmth. It was always hard work and, with heaters blasting and blowing at full power in the car on the way back to the practice, it was another challenge to stay awake, let alone survive evening surgery.

But it's when December arrives that the coldness and snow can really hit. In 2009, arctic weather had the country in a polar grip and frozen weather continued from December through to February. It is the coldest and most prolonged cold spell I can remember in Yorkshire and it made outside veterinary and farming tasks very difficult. Water pipes froze and sheep, or any cattle unlucky enough to still be outside, needed huge amounts of extra food. Some routine vet work was cancelled as collecting areas had morphed into ice rinks. Cows, despite having four feet, are even worse on ice than humans.

"We'll have to put off the blood tests. It's far too slippery in our yard and I don't want the cows slipping and injuring themselves," was a common conversation and equally applicable to other jobs. Emergency work carried on regardless and calvings, lambings, cattle with pneumonia or prolapses or sheep with twin lamb disease became the job for vets who had 4x4s and winter tyres. After one heavy snowfall, a farmer from Hawnby called to arrange a rendezvous with his snow plough, to clear the road to his farm ahead of the vet'nary.

"It's always worse up here," he said, confirming the extreme weather conditions at the top of Sutton Bank. If the wind comes from the north-east, the drifts along the drover's road can obliterate the stone walls and even the road signs. That winter, the piled snow persisted for months.

On another occasion, a colleague appeared back at the practice, ashen-faced after a visit to see a horse above Boltby Bank. It wasn't the unruly yearling that had caused him trauma. He was a diligent vet but a terrible driver and, foolishly, he'd decided to descend the steepest road within miles and lost control. As his Ford Escort went sliding and spinning down the bank, his only option was to save himself by aiming into the snow drift.

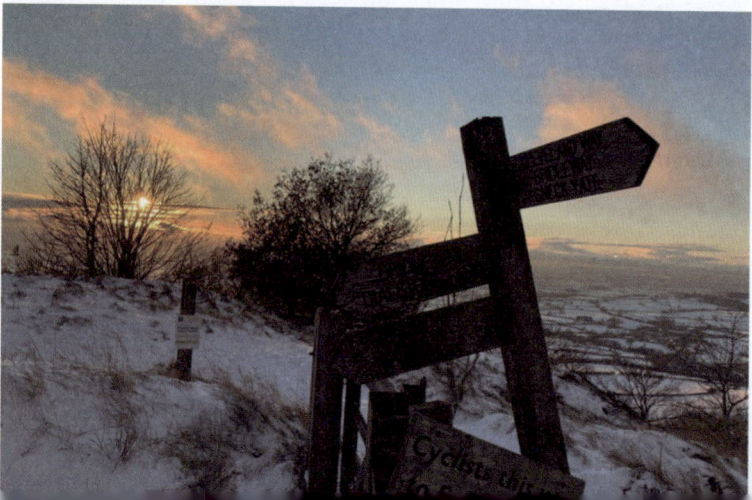

"Pic-a-Nic Baskets?"

The wind was strong and the rain almost horizontal. To be fair, it was hard to tell exactly the angle, being as we were all enveloped inside a cloud. This was not a huge surprise for me, because I've spent a lot of time on the top of the highest point in Yorkshire over the years. Seven hundred and thirty-six metres above sea level doesn't sound massive, but it's high enough to put you in the clouds and at least five degrees colder than the valley bottom. Add in the increased wind speed, it makes the top of Whernside somewhere that most people stop only for as long as the flask of tea remains warm.

The plan that lay before me involved several hours of work, one park ranger called Ian, two assistants, some spades and pick axes, slabs of rock and bags of aggregate. Oh, and two people holding cameras, both of which were pointing at Ranger Ian and me. There was a stone stile that needed to be mended, right on the border between Cumbria and Yorkshire. I'd been invited along to help and get an insight into the work of a Yorkshire Dales ranger. Once again, as well as getting busy with a spade, I was acting as a "presenter" and as far outside any zone resembling comfort that you could imagine.

The first job was to the top. The last time I'd done this, I was wearing Lycra running leggings and running shoes with huge

nobbles underneath, competing in the Three Peaks Race. It was some years ago and was muddy and sweaty. Today's ascent was less strenuous but no less arduous. We clambered into a buggy with newly applied caterpillar tracks, so it felt just like a tank. Picking the route and avoiding the bogs was similar to running up the hill in the race. I hoped Ian knew the way because I had, on occasions, ended up knee-deep in bog having been tricked by the surface conditions. Even with caterpillar tracks, I could picture us sinking, never to be discovered.

Ranger Ian's route proved sensible and safe and we eventually arrived at the top. Ian explained the plan and I grabbed a spade. The cameras started to roll as we began to dig. A reinforced step, on each side of the gap-stile, needed to be made. The ground had eroded, making it hard for anyone who wasn't slimline to squeeze through the gap. It was hard work but an excellent way to keep warm. The poor camera operators weren't having such a good time. Even with a heavy device on your shoulder, it was hard to stay warm, but they fastidiously captured all the action, only occasionally disrupting the important work with (sometimes) relevant questions.

As we dug out the new and improved step, I quizzed Ranger Ian on his work and why it was important. Bizarrely, he was the sole employed ranger in the Three Peaks National Park. Fences, gates, stiles and paths needed constant repair, to enable people to enjoy Yorkshire's wild open spaces while keeping the infrastructure in a decent state. He explained his love for Yorkshire and its wilderness; the cameras zoomed in on his face to capture his passion and enthusiasm, then panned out to get a shot of Ribblehead viaduct in gaps in the cloud. I asked questions where necessary, but most were redundant because Ian was so eloquent. Before long, the early start, hard digging and cold weather made us all hungry, so we sought shelter in the back of the caterpillar truck. As I looked for our packed lunches, I couldn't help but ask Park Ranger Ian if he'd seen the pic-a-nic baskets. Outside of Jellystone and inside a cold, Yorkshire cloud, apparently this wasn't a particularly funny joke.

Hairy Legs

On Tuesday, I confronted some long-standing fears. Natalie, one of our trainee nurses, brought in a few of her exotic pets, to educate and inform some of the staff (the main one being me) and also to help overcome any anxieties induced by slippery snakes, goggle-eyed reptiles or huge and potentially deadly spiders.

We started with Rodney, who was a chameleon, circumspect and friendly. These are peculiar reptiles – their eyes move independently and in all directions and their feet have two toes, rather than four or five like most other quadrupeds. And, of course, they change colour (although disappointingly not necessarily to blend in with the background – Rodney refused to take on the stripes of the towel on the table). But they are not scary, poisonous or dangerous and they will definitely not constrict you to death.

Next, came Eric, curled up in a benign ball with what seemed like a smile on his face. Eric was a banana-coloured (and banana-textured) milk snake and named after Eric Twinge, who turned into Bananaman in the 1980s children's cartoon, after eating the said fruit. I am very frightened of snakes (even ones named after cartoon characters). It's an irrational fear based on lack of proper experience, probably unjustified preconceptions and watching *Indiana Jones* films when I was small. But Eric was not menacing at all and despite his obvious reptile credentials my heart rate remained reasonably steady. I found him quite appealing.

The same could not be said for contestant number three, ("What's your name and where do you come from?") another snake this time draped around Natalie's neck like a thin scarf. Her name was Candy and she came from North America. Nat assured everyone that she was non-venomous and quite friendly, but milk snakes bear a striking resemblance to the deadly dangerous coral snake. This was enough to keep me at a safe distance, but Mark declared himself "not at all frightened of snakes", even if they are brightly coloured and look almost identical to deadly ones. Candy wrapped herself around his neck and, within minutes, started to head down his shirt, tongue flickering all the time and obviously enjoying his aftershave. The worried expression on his face at this point told a very different story and Candy was quickly extricated. Despite this minor trauma for an ophidiophobe like me, the experience so far had been very positive.

Next on the scary list was Rosie, whose name didn't sound scary at all. It was essential the snakes were rehoused, because Rosie was frightened of them and them of her. At last an animal with hair! At last one with legs! Surely, I was back on familiar territory? Sadly, this was not the case, because Rosie had eight legs (and two arms). She had extremely tiny eyes but a HUGE bottom. She was a Chilean rose-hair tarantula and Nat gave us some more details. One was that "we shouldn't handle her if we were worried", because she could give a painful and venomous bite (similar to a bee sting) and could fire irritant hairs at enemies. A quick search of Google informed us all that *tarantulas should be observed, not picked up or handled.*

But Nat was encouraging and nurse Sarah was keen to overcome her own concerns. "If not now, then when?" she reasoned and held out both hands. Before long, they stopped shaking and the beginnings of a smile appeared on her face. Yet another phobia had been expunged, although head nurse Lucy's face wore no trace of a smile when she tried, and my hands were safely enveloped in latex gloves. In conclusion, we all agreed a turn on *I'm a Celebrity* was *definitely* feasible.

Tetanus, Tetanus, One, Two, Three...

We've seen two unusual cases recently, both of the same condition. The exaggerated expressions on each face was the first clue. At first, we all thought they were surprised to see such a lovely, happy, engaging practice, with wonderful welcoming staff. But the dogs' faces remained fixed and unmoving. Normally, dogs relax and quickly become accustomed to their circumstances, but both patients remained tense and surprised. With wide eyes, pricked ears and what looked like a wide grin, which persisted for the duration of the consultation, the diagnosis was fairly easy to make and, fortunately, didn't require a complicated journey through a CT scanner, nor expensive blood tests. In fact, none of the usual advanced imaging or modern tests would be helpful at all.

To cut two reasonably long stories shorter than they were, both dogs were suffering from tetanus. The condition is caused by the neurotoxin derived from a bacterium called *Clostridium Tetani*, a ubiquitous bacterium, with its spores found in soil everywhere. When these spores enter the body, the bacterium releases its potent toxin, where it wreaks havoc by causing muscle spasms.

Horses are particularly susceptible to tetanus, and all horses and donkeys need to be vaccinated regularly against this disease. Dogs, cattle and cats are less prone. I've never seen a cat with tetanus, but I have seen a handful of cows (one of which had swallowed a rusty nail) and a few dogs. But two canine patients within a couple of weeks was unusual. Did it constitute an epidemic? No – I am certain the appearance of two cases was totally coincidental.

I remember the first time I'd ever heard of the disease tetanus. I was about seven. My friend, Jason and I had been digging a hole in some rough land between my house and the main railway line from Castleford to Leeds. I can't remember exactly the purpose of the hole, but I do remember Jason and I using a spade and a garden fork, borrowed from my dad for the job. Jason used the fork to loosen the soil and I'd dig it out using the spade. At the allotted time for dinner (I don't know how us children knew what time dinner time was, because we had no watches and mobile phones hadn't even been thought of, let alone invented), I left Jason to the digging. "I'll be back in a bit," I must have said.

Jason promised to keep working on the hole. "I'll use this fork, 'cos it goes in better," were the last words I heard him say.

After dinner, I returned to find the hole not much deeper than before, two garden tools and no best friend. Jason had gone. I presumed for his dinner too.

Later that afternoon, there was a phone call. It was Jason, apologetically explaining his unauthorised absence from hole-digging duties.

"I had to go to hospital. I was using the fork and I shoved it straight into me foot. It went raight in and it cem raight out the other side. Mam said I needed a tetanus jab, so that's where I've been, at hospital. Anyway, I'm done now so shall we do some more digging?"

Jason was saved from the possibility of certain death, although at that time neither of us had any idea that the condition was anything more serious than a bad nettle sting or a grazed knee.

Forty-odd years later, and I most certainly do realise the seriousness of tetanus. I reckon I've seen half a dozen cases in dogs over my career, and we don't routinely vaccinate dogs against the disease. Interestingly, by comparison, I've never seen a case of distemper.

Both dogs made a full recovery.

Waiting Room Conversations

I came into the conversation halfway through, as I emerged from my consultation room in search of the next patient. I couldn't imagine how it had started.

"Yes, it *is* just like *Mr Benn*," was receptionist Bev's reply to the question I'd missed.

My ears pricked up and I joined in, "*Mr Benn*, as in the children's programme from the 1970s?" I asked, sensing an opportunity to reminisce over pleasures past. It turned out it was *that Mr Benn* and we talked about the classic TV cartoon. Everyone in the waiting room within earshot agreed the show was excellent and that they didn't make television like that anymore. Someone mentioned Bod. Nobody within the discussion could remember exactly where and why Alexander Frog fitted in. (Answers on a postcard please.)

"My favourite was *The Magic Roundabout*," somebody else added.

"Oh, yes. With Florence and Dougal. And Zebedee! Now that was very special!"

By now, more staff had appeared – all younger and blissfully unaware of this TV gold from a prehistoric era – who were oblivious to everything under discussion.

"What on earth are you talking about?" asked nurse Lucy. "And can you check this prescription and have a look at an X-ray?" I gave my apologies and left to get on with my veterinary work, peering at the grey, white and black shades of the X-ray. Lucy headed to a computer, to Google Dougal. Minutes later, she had a smile on her face, confirming that it looked good, adding, "But you didn't *really* watch that? It looks so old!"

Back in the waiting room, happy dogs left, trotting on leads held by happy owners. Pleased mainly because of a cure or sensible plan for the patient, but maybe also because of a pleasant time outside of the consulting room. The waiting room experience is

A stray kitten, looking for a home, prompted some excellent waiting room conversations one day!

an important one and, in my opinion, every bit as crucial as what goes on during the examination or in the operating theatre. I have to say, controversially, that in my opinion the best times were (again from antiquity) when practices held "open surgeries". This haphazard and often chaotic system, just like when we used to go for a haircut, where you arrived and took your turn, could bring a long wait but always led to an interesting conversation with the person (or animal) sitting next to you. Even on a busy day, in a full waiting room, I'd try and get a glimpse of the conversations. It offered a window into the animal owners' world. There was usually an affable atmosphere.

"What are you here for? Chemotherapy? Crikey! He doesn't look poorly at all!" or "What a huge bandage! There must be something really bad going on under there! What a lovely puppy! How old is he?" would be overheard. And regular patients and owners would often meet in passing, if check-up visits coincided, so new friends could follow the progress of recovering pets together.

But the waiting room was not always a friendly place. In my early days as a vet, when established clients only wanted to see the senior partner, just before he hung up his stethoscope and retired, and not the fresh-faced, recently qualified newcomer, a full waiting room meant a sea of averted eyes, whose gaze was swiftly shifted towards the floor whenever I'd call, "Who's next, please?" Eventually, through expediency or empathy, a client would usually stand up and reluctantly make their way to see me, past a row of uncomfortable shuffling pet owners. I'm glad to say, a combination of increasing experience and the now-normal appointment-based system has obliterated this problem. Even though children's television doesn't necessarily get better with time, other things definitely do.

Neospora

I had a phone call from an old friend and former colleague the other day. Ben and I enjoyed some fun times at the start of our mutual careers and we've stayed great friends since those halcyon days when it was a pleasure, a privilege and a thrill to be qualified and working as a vet. We used to marvel in the pub on a Thursday evening – our mutual night off – that we were actually *paid* to do what we'd always dreamed of. Admittedly, we weren't paid very much, but this didn't seem to matter back then. My most valuable worldly possession was my mountain bike and, provided I could pay back my student loan and had enough spare money for a few pints on a night off and fish and chips on the nights when I was on call, then the world was a happy place.

Ben had grander plans though, and moved into the heady world of specialist equine practice. This was a good thing, because I recall his regular advice to dog owners: "Feed him moist green vegetables! Every day!" It was his cure for most conditions. Via a university residency, where he furthered his equine knowledge and gained a collection of letters to go after his name, he headed south. Now he runs his own successful equine clinic and presumably has a healthier bank balance than he did in the late 1990s. He must have, because he's acquired a small herd of belted Galloway cattle and this is why he called me. He explained the situation, describing with great pride how he, an equine vet, had managed successfully to take blood samples from the tail vein of each animal and then submit them to a laboratory to test them for causes of infertility and abortion. But that was where his limited bovine knowledge ran out, and where I came in. Back in the old days, we worked very well together because Ben would do the horse cases and he'd leave any cattle stuff to me. It suited us very nicely, playing to our strengths.

He had sampled the new cows, which had enjoyed some pleasant grazing on his estate (that was the image that I conjured up in my mind, at least) but had not enjoyed a successful calving time. Most of them had lost their calves during pregnancy. Worse news still – every cow had come up positive for a condition called Neospora. This is an unusual disease affecting cattle and dogs. The "Neo" part of the name gives a clue that it is a fairly new and, I think it's still fair to say, poorly understood disease; although maybe it's just poorly understood by me?

In simple terms, it's a bit like toxoplasmosis in sheep. Having written that sentence, I've immediately realised it might not help many readers. The bug is a strange little parasite called a protozoan and spends some of its life inside a dog and the rest in a cow. Dogs don't usually show illness, although I've seen a couple of rare cases where the pesky pathogen can cause neurological disease. It spreads from dog faeces to cattle and that's where most of the disease appears, rendering cattle prone to abortion. Worse still, if calves are born alive and survive, they too can be infected, perpetuating the disease in the next generation. Ben was up to date with the latest horse diseases, but less *au fait* with relatively modern cattle ailments. I could only offer my best advice. To avoid access by dogs to his cattle grazing was already too late. "Ben, I'd suggest that the best cure is to offer them all moist green vegetables." Twenty-five years later, we still shared a laugh at this ridiculous treatment.

Buying Equipment

We've been treating ourselves to new equipment recently. Some have been extras – like the video endoscope, which allows us to look into all sorts of places, inspect ulcers, take biopsies or even remove foreign bodies. It's already been in action to retrieve a whole head of barley from deep in the lungs of a spaniel. It was as satisfying for the surgeon as it was for the dog. Our fancy tonometer, which checks for glaucoma in the eye, is also a welcome new addition. Other purchases have been replacements to update the very basic and second-hand tackle with which we made do in the early months after we opened the Wetherby practice. Without any clients at the outset, we sought out redundant ex-hospital equipment to see us through the early months. The ultrasound machine created superb images, but it was as large and cumbersome as a dalek and took two people to move it around. It's life in a modern veterinary practice was always going to be brief.

Another cheap and temporary stop-gap was the operating light. It may even have been "free to a good home". I hope so, because it emitted lumens at a level similar to a candle and, like the old ultrasound machine, travelled around on rickety wheels. It lived in the corner of theatre and occasionally came into action, though the huge disc-like head would slowly start to droop, so you had to work quickly! With a drooping head, long thin body and ungainly movement, the low-output lamp looked like Jar Jar Binks, the hapless *Star Wars* character. Its replacement arrived last week. It is

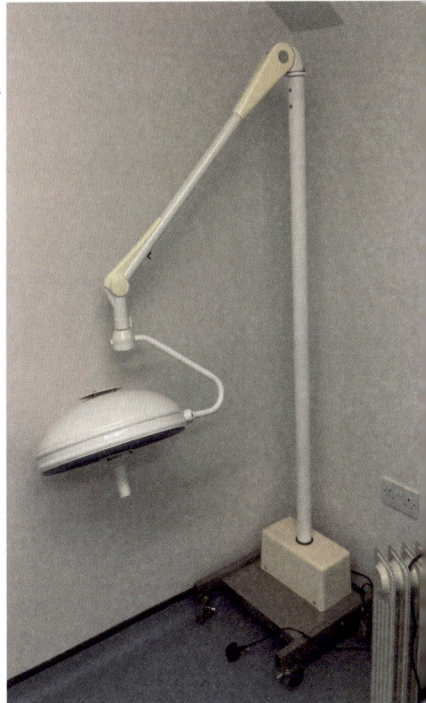

Our old, droopy operating light.

fixed to the wall and, when on full power, you almost need to wear sunglasses. Already it's money well spent.

At the start of my career, I worked with a similarly antediluvian piece of equipment which shared its name with a famous person. The thermocautery machine really should have been in a museum. Its cable had exposed metal ends that were attached by screw-like clamps to the power, which was a cubic wooden box. The handset had a wooden and Bakelite construction and looked exactly like a gun from a 1970s space film. Everyone called it Ronald, as in Ronald Ray-gun! In times of haemostatic crisis, cries of "There's a bleeder. Fetch Ronald!" went a small way to relieve tension during stressful surgery. Eventually, Ronald was consigned to retirement (probably finally finding his place in the museum), thus avoiding a health and safety nightmare. Ronald Ray-gun was replaced by a more modern and nimble thermocautery machine. Accurate and lightweight, it was quickly nicknamed "Ronaldinho" after the sharp-shooting Brazilian football player.

It's a difficult balance starting and running a new business. With no guarantee of clients coming into the waiting room, any sensible new business owner keeps a sharp eye on the outgoings. When I was first a partner, I used to equate every expense to the number of "anal gland equivalents". A new consulting room table, for example, would be approximately two hundred and fifty anal gland expressions. This quick calculation would always focus my mind. But proper equipment is utterly essential to do a decent and proper job. I have not even started calculating how many anal glands will need to be emptied to cover the combined cost of new light, new (and very fancy) ultrasound machine and video endoscope. What I do know though, is that surgery under the powerful spotlight is much easier and that the positive benefits of the scope cannot be overstated. As for the ultrasound machine … it's state of the art and can do everything even the most experienced veterinary ultra-sonographer would need. For my part, the hardest part is switching the blooming thing on!

New Trousers?

I've had plenty of trouser disasters during my veterinary career. Unpredictable discharges of body fluids and semi-fluids have taken their trouser toll. One of the worst disasters occurred when a favourite pair of light-brown cords (probably the comfiest trousers I've ever owned) were washed accidentally with a bright blue fleece. They were rendered a fluorescent turquoise colour, totally incongruous at a veterinary practice. The rescue attempt of repeated washing/boiling left the corrugated velveteen a bright and clinical white. They were more prone to stains than most.

But my most recent calamity came via the fangs of an angry Rottweiler, who came in with a painful sore on his neck.

"He doesn't like face masks," his owner explained. "He gets nervous if he can't see a face properly." It didn't augur well. It turned out he also didn't like vets. And he absolutely hated wearing a muzzle. I inspected Godzilla (not his real name) from a distance at first. Experience told me the lesion was something called *pyotraumatic dermatitis*, a painful, oozing and infected form of superficial skin disease. Infections like this develop almost overnight and are characterised by gluey pus exuding from the skin. The solution is to clip the hair off, clean the area, apply some soothing cream and administer antibiotics to kill the suppurating infection. None of this is possible without the patient being totally unconscious. My cunning plan was to sneak up stealthily on Godzilla and slip an injection into his muscular back leg. I'd leave him with his owners to await the sedative effects of the powerful drugs, which I knew would work well.

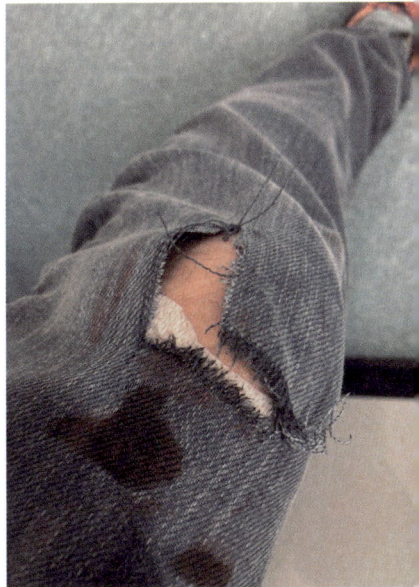

But Godzilla was not so happy with my plan and the huge dog flung his weight around as two owners tried to calm his head end whilst I fumbled with the syringe. Twice the needle bent in the rumpus, but the third attempt looked more promising, until disaster struck. Godzilla swung round, angrily, his teeth bared and saliva flying in long strings from his malevolent jaws. He lunged at me. With no muzzle on Godzilla, and my reactions not as quick as they should have been, I was a sitting duck. Like a scene from a Marvel film, the monster grabbed my leg, wrenching a gaping hole in both my trousers and my flesh.

I couldn't believe my eyes! Blood was pouring from a gash in my knee and soaking into my trousers around the rip in the material. I retired temporarily to the prep room, to let Godzilla calm down and refill my syringe. The next attempt was more successful, and I left Godzilla to fall into a deep sleep, while I attended to my knee. This was the first time I'd been bitten by a dog for many years and I was cross that I'd ended up in this position, not just because of the injury to my trousers and me, but also because of the trauma it had caused the owners and dog. Some antiseptic and a large plaster later, the bleeding had at least abated, but the pain was only just beginning. It ranked with some of the worst bites I'd had over the years. The nastiest was sustained at a dog rehoming charity which I used to visit every week. One emaciated dog, which we'd tried to distract with dog treats so I could administer a vaccine, thought I was trying to steal his precious morsels of food. He sank his teeth into my hand, right across the knuckles. He didn't let go and I've still got the scars. But right now, I had a patient to fix. Under the bandage, I knew my wound would quickly heal and the pain would go. I just hoped Godzilla's sedation was strong!

Godzilla

The sedation I'd injected into Godzilla *was* strong and he slept soundly as I clipped and treated his horrible infection. Underneath the pus, the skin was discoloured with shades of everything from purple to green. As we clipped and cleaned, we chatted about some of the accidents we'd had over the years. Thankfully, bites, kicks, scratches and so on are not that common in a veterinary practice. At least, that's what we tell the health and safety inspector. But, however you look at it, being a vet puts us in harm's way most days. It's impossible to avoid.

Irascible feral cats can be the worse, with too many unpredictable sharp bits to keep contained. I know a veterinary nurse who, many years ago, was the victim of a nasty penetrating bite to her elbow. The stiffness that ensued lasted for almost six months. Cat bites, or even cat scratches, often lead to nasty infections. People rush to the doctor's for an anti-tetanus injection, but the real risk is from sepsis caused by bacteria called pasteurella.

The penetrating injury I once sustained whilst performing a tuberculin test on a herd of cows left me with a similarly lengthy stiffness, luckily of just one finger. It was another accident, pure and simple and unavoidable, when a cow lurched unpredictably. The 4mm needle entered the base of my finger and the gun discharged its contents. Luckily, for all it was painful, I didn't register as a positive reactor, so it could have been worse. Following the MAFF guidelines, I might have been culled.

Treating hind limb injuries in horses is always fraught with risk. One friend of mine said this was the sole reason for his change of career, moving to the safer world of a veterinary pharmaceuticals. "Jules, the thing is, I just got fed up with the constant risk of being kicked in the head," he sighed. We can all empathise. I still recall the chilling time when I felt the air rush past my forehead as the back foot of the sedated yearling skimmed past, before making a hoof-sized hole in the stable door. On that occasion, I decided the small laceration would heal *perfectly well* by secondary intention. I've still got the scar inside my lower lip, where another horse landed its limb with more accuracy one Sunday morning.

But the biggest surge of cortisol came one foggy November day, whilst trying to pregnancy test a herd of suckler cows. The cows most definitely didn't want to be inside a dingy barn. Despite protestations at every point, we steadily made our way through them, ushering them through the cattle crush so I could insert my arm into the rectum of each one in turn. With wild cattle, this can be dangerous enough, as the reluctant patients twist and turn, lurch and dip. You're in a compromised position with your arm shoulder-deep inside a wild cow. And if one coughs at the wrong moment, there's the added danger of becoming splattered in semi-liquid faeces. The last cow did not want to be corralled into the crush and jumped a fence into the barn where the straw bales were kept. I followed. My plan was to shoo it back towards the crush. The cow, intimidated, lowered first her ears, then her head, then pawed the ground like a bull in Spain, then charged at me. For my part, I screamed as my life flashed before my eyes. Luckily, I developed transient superhuman powers and levitated onto the top of a large, round bale. The attacking cow was as surprised as I was. I'd escaped otherwise certain death. As someone once said, it shouldn't happen to a vet. Unfortunately, it often does.

Bike, Van, Ferret

I make notes for myself quite often. Especially in the evening, if there are important things I need to remember the next morning. I'm not a fanatical list-maker, but as my brain grows older and slowly more stupefied, it can be helpful. Anne is a compulsive list-maker. I'm sure I've even seen one item on the daily agenda which said, "Remember to make a list for tomorrow." Maybe I've imagined that.

My list for Monday caused some amusement. All three things on the list were important. It comprised the following words: BIKE VAN FERRET. The new rear mech (aka, rear derailleur) for my bike had arrived and needed to be fitted. With my previously on-site and in-house mechanic now away at university, I needed the help of a local bike shop. The van (second on the list) was the easiest way to get the bike to the shop, which was conveniently close to work. The final item on the list was a stray animal that had been brought into the practice at Thirsk. It was a young, female ferret, which someone had found in their garden. Anne had dealt with it, cautiously because it arrived at the bottom of a very deep cardboard box, which had previously contained some sort of vacuum cleaner. Delving into a dark box with a ferret at the bottom had the potential for calamity, but fortunately there was no incident to report. At least not at this point. The ferret was calmly settled comfortably in a kennel for me (the resident ferret aficionado) to deal with the following day.

I've always loved ferrets. "Fangface", a roguish albino who temporarily lived in a converted wooden filing cabinet, in my parents' garden was my first ever pet. He had a very similar history to the little polecat-coloured female at the surgery. My mate, Mark, turned up on my doorstep one day when I was about ten. I expected him to ask, "Are yer laking out?" as he usually did – it might be football or BMXing, but it would always be "laking". On this happy day, however, Mark didn't want to "lake out". He had found a ferret and wondered if I'd like it. It was one of my childhood dreams come true, and without so much as a single thought about whether this was acceptable to my parents, Fangface was instantly adopted!

But this little polecat – a young female, swiftly christened Jill – could not join the Norton family. With Boris the hapless rabbit in our garden, there was no way she could stay with us.

Jill was happy and healthy, especially after I'd removed her ticks and treated her fleas. She was thin, but ate the food we offered her voraciously and, when I foolishly tried to examine her mouth, demonstrated that her reactions were sufficiently quick and her teeth sharp and penetrating enough to catch her own food.

We put out appeals for the owner, but the week wore on and nobody came forward. After a few phone calls, I managed to arrange a new home for her, with a ferret rescue centre in Otley. Jackie is a lovely lady. She and her husband have devoted decades to rescuing and helping the creatures they love. (Their charity is a wonderful cause, if anyone has any spare pounds to donate, by the way.) We agreed that I would take her over on Monday morning.

On Sunday afternoon, before my tea, I went to check on Jill and get everything ready to take her to her new home. The cute, but increasingly naughty, ferret was delighted to see me with a plate of food and fresh water. She was so delighted that she immediately sank her teeth into my finger again – at least there was no chance I'd forget the third item on my list tomorrow!

Kirby
Wiske

Pateley Bridge

Harrogate